CANADIAN POETRY CHRONICLE
(1984)

CANADIAN POETRY CHRONICLE
(1984)

A Comprehensive Review Of

Canadian Poetry Books

by

DOUGLAS BARBOUR

with an appendix

by

ALLAN BROWN

Quarry Press

Copyedited by Steven Heighton. Designed by Allison Warne.

Canadian Cataloguing in Publication Data

Barbour, Douglas, 1940-
   Canadian poetry chronicle (1984)

ISBN 0-919627-32-3

1. Canadian poetry (English)—20th century—Book reviews.   I. Title.

PS8155.B37 1985   C811′.54′09   C86-090016-9   PR9190.5.B37 1985

Printed in Canada by Tri-Graphic Printing (Ottawa) Ltd.

Published by *Quarry Press, Inc.,* P.O. Box 1061, Kingston, Ontario K7L 4Y5

PREFACE

For over a decade now Douglas Barbour has been reviewing Canadian poetry books yearly and compiling these reviews in his *Canadian Poetry Chronicle*. The *Chronicle* has previously appeared in several periodicals (*Dalhousie Review, West Coast Review,* and *Quarry Magazine*), but this edition marks its first publication as a book.

The book reviews compiled here are comprehensive yet incisive, offering at once an overview of and an insight into the titles at hand. Students and librarians of Canadian Literature will find the *Chronicle* especially useful for informed reading and ordering of poetry books, as will anyone interested in the present state of the art of poetry in Canada.

The *Chronicle* is divided into two major sections: Anthologies and Poetry Books. The reviews are arranged alphabetically according to the author's (or editor's) surname. The Table of Contents follows this pattern to enable easy reference to individual titles. Since Douglas Barbour is a director of Longspoon Press, an Appendix with reviews of books from this press has been written by Allan Brown. An Index of Publishers has also been compiled.

In sum, the book reviews compiled here in the *Canadian Poetry Chronicle* constitute an annotated, critical record of the history of Canadian poetry as it issues from the authors and publishers.

Bob Hilderley
Editor, Quarry Press

CONTENTS

Contents

Contents

Appendix: Longspoon Press Poetry Books

Index Of Publishers

INTRODUCTION

I continue to be impressed, not only by the quantity of poetry being produced, but by the quality of the best work. And here I take issue with a comment of Irving Layton's in a recent interview in *Books in Canada* (March 1984): Layton says that while there's lots of activity, he fails "to see the products, the great poems." He goes on to say that "the competent poem, the workshop poem" which predominates today "lacks passion. It lacks that special feeling, that magic, that transformation, that only a true poet can give to his experience. I can see the poems, but I do not see the poets." *Pace* Layton, I feel that there is a good amount of powerful, imaginative, passionate, and transformative poetry appearing today, although I would add that it tends to come from poets who have hit their stride. Indeed, even the most exciting new writing comes from what can be called older new writers who are publishing their first books in their thirties or forties. But the poetry of transformative power comes from those writers who helped create the explosion of new writing in the 60's and who have continued to grow since then. At any rate, I find enough of it to make this job worthwhile and even truly exciting sometimes.

I tend in some of these reviews to complain of a seeming lack of understanding on the writer's part of the conventions of open form notation and the need to 'score' a poem for rhythmic intensity. In a recent issue of *Open Letter* (Fifth Series, No. 2, Spring 1982), Frank Davey and bp Nichol collaborated on an essay on "The Prosody of Open Verse." A better, clearer introduction to the topic I cannot think of, and I would recommend it especially to young writers who are trying to discover how to make their verses work. It is descriptive, not prescriptive, but I do wish all poets and their readers were possessed of the basic knowledge it offers. I tend to assume a knowledge of what it talks about in my reviews, and have for some years now. But how nice to have the whole thing laid out so neatly and consistently, yet with a full awareness of the ambiguities and inconsistencies which remain.

As should be obvious from the size of this *Chronicle,* I review these books over a long period of time. But at some point I have to stop and get a ms off to Quarry Press. So some 1984 books will have to wait for 1985. The other point I wish to make is that the "I" reviewing changes over time, too; so, in fact, you are reading a review by a number of reviewers, all named Douglas Barbour, and not all in total agreement with each other. This may make for some contradiction; I hope it also makes for interesting reading.

1

ANTHOLOGIES AND MISCELLANEOUS WORKS

Any anthology reflects its editor's tastes, but George Bowering's four volume *The Contemporary Canadian Poem Anthology* (Coach House Press, 1983) is exemplary in this regard. Each volume contains five poets: I: Margaret Atwood, bill bissett, Robin Blaser, George Bowering, Victor Coleman; II: Frank Davey, Christopher Dewdney, Brian Fawcett, D.G. Jones, Lionel Kearns; III: Robert Kroetsch, Daphne Marlatt, David McFadden, Barry McKinnon, John Newlove; IV: bp Nichol, Michael Ondaatje, George Stanley, Fred Wah, Phyllis Webb, plus essays on poetics by Bowering, Marlatt, Nichol & Davey, and Webb (Nichol & Davey's is a reprint of the essay mentioned above in the *Introduction*). This list contains many expected figures, but what makes the whole anthology so worthwhile are the unexpected or lesser known poets. I am sorry there are only three women among the twenty poets, and believe Sharon Thesen, at the very least, would fit in very well indeed.

Nevertheless, the anthology contains a fine selection of each poet's work, and it takes a stance vis à vis the *act* of writing poetry which I can only applaud. In other words, what Bowering has to say in his introduction strikes me as eminently sane and fair, and is a statement I wouldn't mind signing my own name to:

> The public & political hoopla meant almost nothing to the invention of the poetry you will find represented in this book. Diverse as they are, there is one thing these twenty poets hold in common, that being the assumption or belief that the animator of poetry is language. Not politics, not nationalism, not theme, not personality, not humanism, not real life, not the message, not self-expression, not confessions, not the nobility of work, not the spirit of a region, not the Canadian Tradition — but language. The centre & the impetus, the world & the creator of poetry is language.
>
> The poets of contemporary Canada are many & varied. Some are stubborn, & some are even stupid. Some join large groups not on the basis of what they believe about poetry but because they have published some. Some even think that language is a tool used by a poet to get a job done. But the poets in this anthology are agreed that the poet must not fancy himself so much as to abrogate a power over language, language their elder & better. Like children again, they know enough to be seen & not heard, to let language, which knows so much more than they do, speak. Language, in this case English, is not spoken. It speaks.

For most dedicated readers of Canadian poetry, the selections from Atwood, Bowering, Davey, Jones, Kearns, Kroetsch, Marlatt, McFadden, Newlove, Ondaatje, and Web should contain no surprises. And even bissett, Coleman, Nichol, and Wah have gained a fair amount of notice. But to also have the brilliantly illuminated texts of Blaser and Dewdney, the politically rooted lyrics of Fawcett, McKinnon, and Stanley, and especially to have all these poets together, juxtaposed in their various dedication to the poetic ideal Bowering has enunciated, is something of a lesson in itself. For, despite the implicit impression that these poets will be alike, their work demonstrates how wide-ranging the possibilities of such a poetic are.

For those of us who were not there, the reprint of a famous magazine provides a pot-pourri of emotions: instant nostalgia for what we never knew; fascination in seeing the poets we now know so well working together in comparative anonymity; pleasure in what they actually achieved in their youth. As it turns out, little magazines often have an influence over the years far beyond what their original circulation would suggest was possible; and that is certainly the case with *CIV/n*. Thus, the appearance of *CIV/n: A Literary Magazine of the 50's* (Véhicule Press, 1983), edited by the original editor, Aileen Collins (with the assistance of Simon Dardick), is an event to be welcomed. Accompanied by Michael Gnarowski's "Index", Collin's "Introduction" and Irving Layton's "Recalling the 50's" — both of which suggest the excitement and camaraderie of the venture — Ken Norris's "The Significance of *CONTACT* and *CIV/n*," as well as some wonderfully evocative photographs, the book is a huge feast.

Reading the actual reprints is great fun. There is early work by Leonard Cohen, Eli Mandel, Louis Dudek, Phyllis Webb, Robert Creeley, Raymond Souster, Irving Layton, Gael Turnbull, D.G. Jones, Charles Olson, and others. Many of these poems have become familiar, but there are also many, especially from poets as self-critically astute as Webb, which did not make it into permanent collections. Equally interesting are the essays and reviews, which provide insights into the opinions and poetic theories these writers held at that time. But what is present on every page — in the art, in the verse by writers who failed to grow and those who did grow far beyond these youthful effusions, in the obvious pleasurable effort of producing each issue, and in the handful of memorable poems — what is present is the energy and enthusiasm of all those who were involved in and committed to this mug's game of poetry. *CIV/n* is not simply an important book for students of the period, it is also a delight to read.

Steel Valley (Aureole Point Press, 1984) is, I believe, the first chapbook from James Deahl and Bruce Meyer's very small press. Both men have contributed poems on Pittsburgh (whence, I assume, they originally came to Canada), and Gilda Mekler has contributed the linoleum cuts and a full colour reproduction of a painting titled "River Iron." It's a lovely chapbook, entirely set in letter press and so reminding us of the glories

that once were. Meyer's and Deahl's poems recollect images from Pittsburgh's past and hold them in (at least implied) ironic contrast with the
present. Both poets tend to work a traditional iambic blank verse line, and
a clear Romanticism informs their vision of the city of steel. *Steel Valley*
is a finely made introduction to Aureole Point Press and its artists.

The aptly titled *New Romantics* (*Cross Country*, # 16, 1983) contains just
three poems, David McFadden's "Night of Endless Radiance," Ken Norris's
"Acts of the Imagination," and Jim Mele's "The Art of Discovery." They
are all fascinating attempts to express what editor Mele calls "the recognition
that imagination is the unifying force in our lives, that it is the common
ground of our humanity." Meles seems to think that those poets whose
frames are "the 'particular,' the intellectually surreal, or 'the word as object,'"
no longer serve that recognition, but I would argue that it's only the poor
practitioners who so fail their origin.

McFadden's poem is the most successful in realizing the editor's desire.
The second of at least three "Kootenay Sonatas" (the first is *A New Romance*,
the third, *Country Of The Open Heart*), "Night of Endless Radiance" finds
McFadden entertaining what is surely a high-Romantic notion once again:
that there is a discourse of transcendence and that we can all speak and
hear it if we would but try. In McFadden's case, such a discourse will
be, of course, comic and awe-full at once, and as he seeks to express "the
ordinary radiance of the heart," he slips and slides from high to low and
back again, plays marvelous punning tricks, and makes a genuine effort
to show us that "The mind is a diamond/the size and shape of the holy
grail." I recommend this poem, but only to those who read it as the link
between *A New Romance* and *Country Of The Open Heart* — the first marks
the marvelous beginning of this new kind of writing from McFadden, the
latter takes what is still tentative in "Night of Endless Radiance" and realizes
its potential in full glory. All three mark something very special in
McFadden's *oeuvre*.

Ken Norris's "Acts of the Imagination" is Book Three of his continuing
work, *Report on the Second Half of the Twentieth Century*. It has much in common
with McFadden's poem, though lacking its transcendental humour, replacing
placing it with the sexual longing that is so much a part of all Norris's
poetry. It celebrates what its title signals, and does so in terms of one
of the oldest of all conflicts, night versus day. It has many marvelous
moments but, unlike McFadden's poem, is also clearly didactic in its
approach to its materials. It is argumentative, seeking to win us to its point
of view.

Mele's poem is also an argument, this time from history and concerning
the discovery of new lands which leads to baffled control rather than
understanding entrance(ment). The most singlemindedly intellectual of the
three poems, it advances an argument from within the belly of the beast
which Dennis Lee and George Grant would find valid. Because of its rigorous

argumentation, it is less moving than the other two poems, but it certainly repays attention.

New Romantics is a fine introduction to new work from three interesting writers which argues the case of the imagination with fervour and devotion.

I once wrote an essay on Louis Dudek titled "Poet as Philosopher," in which I argued that his poetry insisted on being an act of the mind as much as an act of the heart. Indeed, Dudek's poetry tends to give priority to reason. It is not surprising, then, to find that Dudek's latest book is called *Ideas for Poetry* (Véhicule Press, 1983) and is a collection of aphoristic prose pieces which explore ideas Dudek feels could feed one's poetry. Prefaced by a comment of Yeats "that the only way in which poetry can be philosophical . . . is by portraying the emotions of a soul dwelling in the presence of certain ideas," Dudek's book seeks to entertain a variety of ideas on everything from art to zoology. Here, for example, is Dudek on "Opinion":

> There are only two authentic tests of poetry, your own enjoyment of it (for the present) and the test of time.
>
> All awards, publicity and popularity are mere noise that distracts you from your own response; these things have little correlation with the verdict of posterity.
>
> In short, anything that interferes with your own judgement, with the judgement of the individual, is a bane to literature.

and on "Meaninglessness and Meaning":

> A "meaningless difference" as the source of significant events is the principle that underlies the logic of chance. That is why many thinkers — Einstein among them — have refused to acknowledge chance as a fundamental principle of nature. But if "meaningless difference" is a principle that leads us to the most meaningful results, if that is indeed a key to the creative process of the universe, who are we to cavil at the order of nature?

What Dudek seeks to do in these (rather opinionated, but then if they weren't they wouldn't really be that interesting) pieces is to provoke the kind of thinking he feels poetry shouldn't be without. His little book may not succeed exactly in doing that, but it should get its readers thinking and arguing, and that in itself is worthwhile.

As a kind of addendum to their anthology *Cross/Cut,* Ken Norris and Peter Van Toorn have edited *The Insecurity of Art: Essays on Poetics* (Véhicule Press, 1982), a collection of twenty-five essays by English-language Québec poets on aspects of their craft. One thing that emerges quickly is that there's no easy agreement among these writers. John Glassco rails against poetry readings while Tom Konyves celebrates performance poetry; Robert Allen attacks field poetics while Ken Norris, Stephen Morrisey, and Richard Sommer defend variations of them. Other essays, like Dudek's are historical, or, like Anne McLean's are polemical. All are interesting, although a reprint of Irving Layton's "Preface to *The Tightrope Dancer"* seems unnecessary.

The Insecurity of Art is almost always provocative (Anne McLean's essay on a post-feminist poetics is especially so, and witty to boot), but it is not in any way a unified text on poetics. This is probably right and proper: poets tend to be highly individualistic, and what the editors manage to demonstrate in this collection is that contemporary poets in Québec are pursuing their craft in many different ways and are able and willing to discuss their practice with intelligence and style.

POETRY BOOKS

Dig Up My Heart: Selected Poems 1952-83 (McClelland & Stewart, 1983) is Milton Acorn's second Selected; his first, *I've Tasted my Blood* is famous because it *did not* win the Governor General's Award and therefore received — from a group of fellow poets — the first Canadian Poetry Award. But Acorn kept writing and publishing, eventually winning the Governor General's Award in 1975 for *The Island means Minago,* which is generously represented in this new Selected.

Acorn is, of course, something of a legend, and though his life, back in his beloved Prince Edward Island, is quieter now, he has lost none of the fire which raged through his early work. Indeed, some of the new poems in *Dig Up My Heart* are more passionately apprehensive of life and nature than ever. This is a rich and diverse collection of poems by a Romantic lyric poet whose revolutionary passion would have warmed the hearts of Shelley and Byron.

Indeed, one of the things I felt while reading *Dig Up My Heart* was that Acorn achieves the kind of lyric intensity Layton speaks of and strives for more often than Layton himself does, perhaps because Acorn's outward yearning compassion is greater than Layton's. At any rate, whether writing of his family, of natural beauty, of sexual passion, of work and the fight for a fair return, or even of American imperialism (but these are his least successful pieces), Acorn creates poems of stinging intensity, and true lyric power. I believe these lines from "A Sword of Steel" succinctly sum up his continuing efforts:

> What am I now, this instant, without
> you? reader? lover? person in a crowd?
> My poems are one long varitoned shout
> to reach you and get an echo.
> They are as well a listening
> to land amidst your stir and hear you sing.

The song continues no matter how hard the wordly world of capitalism, deceit, and envy tries to drown it out, and Acorn listens and joins in.

All the famous early poems are here, and welcome: "Knowing I Live in a Dark Age," "The Natural History of Elephants," "I've Tasted My Blood," and many others. From Part Two, some deeply felt meditations on war as it affected/afflicted the people of PEI, some aching love poems, a number of mythico-historical statements, and some wisely comic portraits stand out. The title poem, the last one in the book, is pure Acorn in its wild assertions, its passionate claiming, its resolution. It brings to a ringing close a book chockfull of powerful poetry, summing up a life lived in beauty's pursuit, and far from over yet:

> Dig up my heart from under Wounded Knee
> Where it's been living as a root in the ground
> Whispering the beat, to fool mine-detectors.
> Though there may not be much Indian in me
> That fraction was here first. It's senior.
> That this heart to grow a man around.
>
> I shall be Heartman — all heartmuscle!
> Strong and of longest endurance
> I've acted, thought and dreamt to nurse my will
> Proud for the day of the People's Judgement
> When vision rides again and all that's meant
> Is said and flashed from eyes once thought blind
> Fewer and fewer of us, rest now in silence.

Margaret Atwood's *Murder in the Dark* (Coach House Press, 1983) is subtitled "Short Fictions and Prose Poems." A great argument could be made that these are the forms most amenable to Atwood's particular vision, that in them she can do what she does best even better. Atwood is a master of the aphoristic, and these pieces punch home the paradoxical power of aphorism, whether they are clearly narrative, like the wittily science-fictional "Simmering," or more purely parabolic, like "Iconography." In her novels, Atwood occasionally seems to have given herself too much space; the force of her vision is dissipated in the extensions of conventional realism, in a kind of longwindedness that muffles her essential insights. The fictions of *Murder in the Dark* will frustrate those who read only her novels because these pieces refuse to bend to the conventions and approach the poetic.

One of the major pleasures this book offers is its continuing interrogation of its own fundamental means, for many of the selections hold up language itself to analytical investigation. Since language is how we know our world, its devious conventions of reference can make that world one way or another. Atwood's caustic comic sensibility plays with these conventions, discovering their faults, their failures. Most often, these discoveries have a feminist base, but other aspects of the politics of linguistic repression come under fire, too.

Yet this is not a despairing book. Some pieces are in fact celebratory; and even those which examine some of the worst possibilities are energetic and vital in their performance. A few are just easy jokes. On the whole, however, *Murder in the Dark* is one of Atwood's more successful works of prose — because it is also, very specifically, a work of the poetic imagination.

Rereading Margaret Avison's first two books, now collected in one volume, *Winter Sun/The Dumbfounding: Poems 1940-1966* (McClelland & Stewart, 1982) I was reminded of just how great her poetry is. We all know the anthology pieces, or should, and they deserve the prominence they have been given, if only because they are among her most immediately approachable works, but the rest comprise a major *oeuvre*, and McClelland & Stewart should be congratulated for bringing it back into print for a new generation of readers.

Winter Sun was an astonishing work when it appeared, and remains a stunning achievement today. "Nobody stuffs the world in at your eyes. / The optic heart must venture: a jail-break / And re-creation." Although her specifically Christian faith has deepened in the work that followed, Avison has remained true to this call for vision. If in *The Dumbfounding* the vision is wholly grounded in the Gospel, it nevertheless remains one which encounters "the world" always, seeing even the tiniest "narrow winged / long-elbowed-thread-legged / living insect" as one of God's creatures to be celebrated in a poem.

Avison has been called a twentieth-century metaphysical poet, and insofar as a brilliant intelligence and much learning informs her poetry, the description is valid. But she is also a naïve yet spirited and spiritual fabulist, a poet of immediate perceptions, and the possessor of a superb ear for the rhythmic subtleties of contemporary poetics. Her language ranges widely and demonstrates high erudition, yet she can use the simplest speech effectively. She is a master of craft, but craft in her work always serves vision.

Avison's is a poetry which you can return to again and again. Its rich resonances and compassionate commitment to the world (God's world, she tells us) reward each reading with further insights. And, as the final poem in the book insists, it reminds us of what we too easily forget or ignore, what is "Unspeakable" only because we do not try hard enough to speak it; but she notices, she pays attention as only a poet does, and she finds the proper speech:

> The beauty of the unused
>   (the wheatear among birds, or
>   stonechat)
> the unused in houses (as a
>   portion of low roof swept by the
>   buttery leaves of a pear tree
>   where a manx cat is
>   discovered-just now-blinking his
>   sunned Arctic sea-eyes in the
>   sun-play)
> the beauty of the
>   unused in one I know, of
>   excellent indolence
>   from season into
>   skywide wintering
> should be
> confidently, as it is
> copious and new into the morning
> celebrated.

Poetry, like prayer, is perhaps a significant example of the unused. Even those who do not share Ms. Avison's beliefs will find in her poetry a beauty worthy of the finest celebration.

As I once noted in my review of *The Terrible Word*, William Bauer has a terrific (Yankee) sense of humour which seems to be suited to his adopted home of New Brunswick (for we well know that the Eastern states and provinces share a basic Puritan heritage, the only cure for which is an earthy irony). Such a sensibility is on display once more in *Unsnarling String* (Fiddlehead Poetry Books, 1983) which contains two sequences, "Everett Coogler" (originally published as a chapbook) and the title poem, plus a number of shorter works.

"Everett Coogler" is a decidely Yankee poem, and its setting in baseball-conscious Hamsterville points up its roots. Coogler is an old codger, whose trials and tribulations usually find him winning when he appears to lose if only because he is the bright underside of the American dream: he uses all his wit to avoid mere material success. As an eccentric, Coogler's a nifty character, and represents the kind of comic-persona poetry Bauer has mastered.

The first of the shorter pieces, "Ceremony," shows this persona at its best. Its thirteen sections are fragments of the speech of a man who has built a little city of toothpicks and invited his friends over to celebrate its completion. It is typical of Bauer that this speech is at once absurd and his *apologia pro vita sua* as an artist. The final section is ambiguously poised: "Yes, I worry about fire — / And yet I made it / Highly flammable / Didn't I?" "Truant Officer Poems" also show Bauer's love for those whom society dislikes yet who help maintain it. A number of the other poems, especially "A True Account" and the "Tantrum Poems," had me laughing out loud.

As did the title sequence, but in "Unsnarling String" Bauer posits himself as protagonist and presents a lost cause as the comic image of all "useless" endeavour (again he has found a humorous, (photo-) negative sign for art which carries the weight of truth). It's the best thing in the book, full of nuance and delightful paradox. And it reveals Bauer as a genuinely comic poet, a writer who will surely entertain you with his stories and leave you feeling a bit better than when you opened his book.

In *A Heart of Names* (Mosaic Press, 1983) Robert Billings eschews the larger historical questions of his previous book *The Elizabeth Trinities* to delve into domestic inheritances. These are poems of grandfathers and grandmothers, of parents, and of the growing family to which he now belongs.

The opening sequence, "Cayuga," takes moments out of the distant familial past as they happened, and in the telling present them as they are recalled. The poem is deceptively simple in its straightforward narration and lack of obvious tropes. The poems in "A Ring of Stones" are essentially occasional, ranging from dream visions and historical reveries to love poems and a quietly understated elegy for his father. Usually lyrically precise, they only occasionally dissipate their energy in weak similes. "Fruit Cellar Poems" is a short sequence on creativity and its origins. Here the poet literally roots himself in the ground and routes his imagination through it. He is aware of the incongruities of descending beneath the house to compose, yet insists "I come here to be closed in / and to open."

Closed in by memory and history, Billings nevertheless continues to open his imagination to the possibilities of the ongoing poem. *A Heart of Names* shows a young poet continuing to hone his talent and grow in his craft.

Billings' *Trying to Dream for My Son* (Aureole Point Press, 1984) is the second handsome chapbook from this new small press. In it Billings performs a number of deliberately Romantic gestures as poet, lover, and father. Two poems pay specific homage to Robert Lowell and Sylvia Plath — grandly Romantic in their poetic gestures, themselves, especially in their personalism — by having the speaker read those poets' works in particular places. This act provides a sense of poetic vocation which supports the meditation on imagination(s) that is the title poem.

In these poems, nature, even in storm, is desirable; humanity's war against nature and itself echoes across lakes and through bad dreams, and only rain on the lake, music, love can be held against the destruction. The vision is not new but Billings makes it his, here, especially in the title poem. I feel a few of the poems could be tightened up, some similes rendered into more powerful metaphors, but on the whole this is a good example of its kind of poetry.

Seagull on Yonge Street (Talonbooks, 1983) is bill bissett's latest collection (he has published more than fifty now) and like most of the others it is a mixture of weird narratives, love lyrics, sharp images, chants, concrete poems, and drawings. Although I wouldn't want to compare them on other grounds, bissett is like Irving Layton in that he writes prodigiously and publishes everything; both poets will eventually be served by good editors who will sift the wheat from the chaff of their effusions.

Seagull on Yonge Street is a big book, with far more long narrative poems than usual, some of which, like "answering servis," are almost full-fledged short stories. But because it's so large and varied a collection, it's too bad that one of bissett's most simplistic examples of political didacticism, "Mr president dont yu know yr an," appears right at the beginning. bissett is really a post-Romantic writer in the Shelleyan vein, and like Shelley he sometimes offers rants in the place of poetry, but he also shares with his precursor a visionary sense of humanity as potentially free on earth. That vision shines through in many of these poems. In a poem about an accident victim, he says "i walk away   shakee from n strongr / for the communyun sumtimes hauntid by the undrdressing uv th / bodee   what it alone   cant tell us with soul   but with / miracul uv its entree   n workings in this world." bissett's great gift in the physical body of his poems is to reveal that miracle in its many, shifting guises.

bissett remains an incorrigible idealist even as he tells us once again how people in power have been corrupted and seek to destroy what he loves. One of his saving graces is his sense of humour when confronted by the absurd. A wide-eyed innocent, apparently, he simply writes down what he sees and thinks. The carefully crafted naïveté of his vision reveals a world we would sometimes prefer to ignore but which we can't deny. We should be glad he continues to share his perceptions with us.

Robin Blaser's *Syntax* (Talonbooks, 1983) seeks a larger order than words can provide yet the poet is consistently confronted by the fact that it's only *in* words that any order he can conceive will be found. The last, and longest, piece, "lake of souls," is sub-titled "reading notes," and in a way that's exactly what the whole book is. Blaser, a learned poet if ever there was one, reads the world as he reads his many books, and in both texts he finds material for these poems of mysterious clarity.

The voices in *Syntax* are many and varied, from Romantic poets to recent critics, from anonymous tombstone carvers and janitors to historical and religious scholars. All have something to say within the larger pattern of inquiry Blaser is constructing here. As he says in the Preface: "I read, walk, listen, dream, and write among companions. These poems do not belong to me." Note that writing comes *after* the other pursuits, it follows upon them. In these poems of cosmic laughter and troubling thought, Blaser pays these other voices the supreme compliment of getting out of their way and copying them clearly. Their concerns are important: life, death, violence, the sacred (if it can still be found), and human mystery. Blaser's own sense of rhythmic attention gives prose a new poetic intensity, but he is also willing to quote 40 lines of Shelley in the midst of his own notations since all these voices (and his own, though present in some of the poems, is granted no privilege) are equal in their recognitions of the world they speak. It is a world in which much has happened and been articulated; myths and legends, tales and poems, metaphysics and metamorphoses — all are to be found in the patterns of discourse which make up *Syntax*.

"Image-Nation 16 (anaclitic variations" is a good example of the poet's method, filled as it is with voices and hints of voices, a chorus of imaginative possibilities we are asked to entertain:

> a lean to   and
> it is true *the stars fell into language*
> so many   *Guesses at Heaven*
> throng in the air, we come upon them
> now and again
>
> he bathed in the dragon's blood
> but a leaf of the linden stuck to
> his skin   the weak spot at the beginning
> "a-dieu," he said, "out of the golden-
> tongued nightmare"
>
> the real condition of light drinks
> from the fingers   fooling the bees,
> just as we drink from cups
> and gold, wandering
>
> the name-of-the-game is interpretable,
> but   *not to be named is to be lost*
> *in light*
>   (phrases from Geoffrey Hartman and Keats)

Syntax won't be to everyone's taste but I find it liberating in its refusal of lyric egotism, in the way it seeks, through an extreme textuality, to achieve the vision Yeats speaks of in his last poems, "Lapis Lazuli," for example. It is a noble and far-sighted book.

The title of Marianne Bluger's second book, *On Nights Like This* (Brick Books, 1984), implies much about the attitudes to be found in her poems. "On nights like this, you gotta be prepared for anything." Exactly, and Bluger's poems recognize with grace and wit that "Something like nothing / You've ever seen descends / some mornings," which puts us "with that Greek who marvelled / at the stars and so doing fell / into a pond, a night, an end, / his own especial sea / weird with reality."

Bluger

What delights in these poems is the way they juxtapose "especial" visions with a "weird" but undeniable "reality." The domestic and the fantastic live comfortably side by side here, whether memory or imagination brings them together (and who, really, is to tell the two apart). "Grandmother" is a good example of Bluger's particular gifts:

> Huge women reigned from parlour chairs
> in the era when there still were queens,
> or took to the sea as captains,
> anchored with skeins — apron and petticoat
> were sail and means. Maternal women these
> juggling cast-iron skillets on spit-hot stoves, or
> baking twenty loaves while the last,
> glass rows of amber jelly, mincemeat, marmalade
> set for legendary meals.
>
> They did their wash on Mondays in a crank machine
> that slopped hot suds on the linoleum,
> then grabbed a string mop, calling to the hands
> to swab and fill the wood-box up.
> 'If you're bored, Jane, work your quilt,
> or get the first load off the line.' Superb
> their part was — something fine.
>
> Sometimes I too stay in all day and darn
> or bake an ovenful of pies, or shine the brass
> or speak firm, gentle reason to the children.
> But then the ragged macaw on my shoulder claws
> and bawls: 'The captain's on the deck
> but it's Thursday just the same.' And waves
> pass over me of 20th century sea sickness.
> I work the needle fast on the torn sail so
> my hands won't shake. And pray and make
> these poems to translate how we live:
> in a small craft of unregistered fleet,
> with no chart or riches in the hold.
>
> I hear the other women
> adrift in their boats;
> they are singing a chorus,
> the only word of which I catch
> is 'Grandmother'.

But it doesn't stand alone. At times Bluger reminds me of Colleen Thibaudeau, but she is no copier. She has already, in this early book, staked a claim for the particularities of her own vision. It's one I hope to be able to share again.

A Selected Poems should, among other things, offer a general overview of the major themes and modes of a poet's work and sift out the weaker verses, leaving the best to shine in each other's company. The Selected half of *The Sunday Before Winter: The New and Selected Poetry of Marilyn Bowering* (General Publishing, 1984) does just that, and its 75 pages offer a sharper, more precise vision of Bowering's particular graces as a poet than any of her individual volumes has done. The lengthy selection of new poems has the same balance of good and weak verse as any other single collection.

Robin Skelton says "the world that we touch and the world that we dream are brought together" in Bowering's poetry, and, indeed, it is her effort to bring them together that accounts for the fairy-tale quality of many of her fragmented fables. They feel like speeches the characters in supernatural ballads or tales might make, but sometimes they are so severed from a possible context they fail to engage me in their putative emotional conflicts. When she does suggest enough of the various characters' backgrounds, however, the poems cut like a cleaver, as in one of her earliest poems, the first in this volume, "Rose Harbour Whaling Station 1910," where the title provides a solid base from which the monstrous imaginings of the poem can take flight.

The longest selection in the first part of the book is from her last volume, *Giving Back Diamonds*, which I believe is her best. A sardonic humour plays across her magic incantations, rooting them in the phenomenal world more securely than before. Some of the new poems achieve this grounding too, although others seem to strive too hard for mystery only to achieve opaqueness. I especially liked "A Pregnant Woman Travelling Alone," where the mystical, even religious, allusions all have comic roots in the fact of pregnancy and its concommitant social difficulties. Bowering will write lines or stanzas which pierce the mind with their intensely felt figures, but I still find the whole poem not quite reaching me. Those that do reach me have a haunting quality that guarantees they will stick in the mind. An especially haunting poem, because of its deceptive simplicity, is "Love Poem for Lin Fan," for which I'd gladly trade all of the more strident attempts at mysterioso:

> No bud is so delicate as your tongue tip.
> The sun has stopped.
> The moist rock breathes for you.
> A murmuring of blood is in my ears, in the wind.
> When you awake, mist covers you.
> Down here, in the forest,
> We are still.
>
> My mind goes no further.

The Sunday Before Winter is a good introduction to the work of a poet who continues to mature in her craft and who has already created some powerful examples of the poetry of dream spells and waking trances, of the mind caught between beauty and terror.

Robert Bringhurst's *The Beauty of the Weapons: Selected Poems 1972-82* (McClelland & Stewart, 1982) thoroughly deserved the honour of being short-listed for the Governor-General's Award for its year. Aside from *Bergschrund* in 1975, most of Bringhurst's publications have been in very limited editions, which means that until this volume, few readers had a chance to evaluate a good selection of his work. In the light of *The Beauty of the Weapons*, Bringhurst must be judged an extraordinary poet, one of the finest of his generation, the creator of a poetry which achieves what he himself calls in a poem, "the quality of crystal, / clarity's nature, / . . . the stricture / of uncut, utterly / uncluttered light."

In a previous *Chronicle* I raved about "the passionate, intellectual experience" the poems of *Bergschrund* offered their readers. Since that time, Bringhurst has expanded the range of his palette, while the precision, clarity, and power he achieves have grown more profound. A learned writer, with a knowledge of half a dozen languages and an obviously wide experience of many texts from the past, he also has a sharp eye for physical and emotional details. If many of his poems emerge from earlier texts, they also speak with their own new voices. The poet finds in the lines and speech of earlier people much that can speak to us today. Thus his series of high intellectual comedies on various pre-Socratic philosophers, for whom he obviously feels empathy. But he can also put on the persona of Jacob, in a long poem of powerful questioning, or that of Petrarch facing death and meditating his will into being in a poem of beautifully felt friendship and grace.

Even as he seems to be inventing new tales, as in the extraordinary "Bone Flute Breathing," with its insistence of the violence implicit in art and love, the ghost of an ancient archetypal tale hovers over the lines. And then, when he takes on one of the most famous mythic encounters, that of "Leda and the Swan," he renews it through savage arguments with earlier versions, especially Yeats'. Orpheus can be found questioning his task or being questioned by it, too, not to mention many other famous sages and singers. Bringhurst stakes his claim to membership in such a company by invoking and confronting its members. Their voices swell his chorus, but the reader recognizes it is *his* chorus always.

There is much to admire and enjoy in this volume, from the severely intellectual poems of the early years to the strangely lyrical yet violently aware poems on the vagaries of love which fill out the second half of the book. Most of Bringhurst's poems are too long to quote, but "Poem Without Voices" (despite the fact that here as elsewhere it is the various and vigorous voices which make the poem so intriguing; but perhaps this title points

to the lyrical quality of the poem — without *other* voices, it implies) provides
a glimpse of his abilities:

> The light that blooms in your body
> blooms in my hands. Around us the ground
> is strewn with its petals.
>
> I have seen on a street in Guadalajara
> wind set the petals of a jacaranda
> down on the ground surrounding a pine.
>
> Love, this is evergreen. Let it be.
> You will see, they fall also. Listen
> again: the silences.
>
> ripen
> deep in the sullen beaks
> of the intricate wooden flowers.

The Beauty of the Weapons is one of the necessary books. That it is a
continually stimulating, provocative delight to anyone interested in language and how it can sing goes without saying. The extraordinary oxymoron
of the title says something about the nature of poetry which the poems
themselves never let us forget. This book is a feast.

The three sequences in Allan Brown's *Locatives* (Nebula Press/Quarry
Press, 1982) all perform as the title implies: they locate their speakers,
spiritually. Brown's work has been noted for the way it reflects a 'seeking
mind,' for its intellectual rigor, and for its verbal complexity, but *Locatives*
reveals with great clarity how much he owes to the great Romantics and
their spiritual quests, especially in the form of the ode.

The sequences in *Locatives* are not quite odes but they are ode-like, and
as they move from "Nocturne Sequence," with its apprehension of "The
bitter fluid of loneliness," through "Lunations," which, despite its memories
of physical delight in youth, also seems to focus most on "the lost/thing
almost plain," to "La Corona: A Marian Octave," in which the birth of
Christ offers some hope of light in the dark night of the soul, they figure
forth a journey in which much is despairingly lost but much is also hopefully
gained.

Brown's syntax is often convolute and crabbed, reflecting the twists and
and turns his imagination takes as it faces its quandaries. But there are
lines of sudden and sharp awareness, lines of precise physical apprehension
which sing with positive clarity. Though not for everyone, *Locatives* proffers
a particular spiritual sensibility in its difficult yet moving gesture of
something very like prayer.

This year's *Winter Journey* (Quarry Press, 1984), with its Introduction by W.J. Barnes and afterword by Brown himself, is an altogether larger undertaking, a gathering of poems (some of which appeared in Brown's first book) meant to define the concerns and obsessions his work has focussed upon so far. Indeed, he argues that the act of gathering, revising, and finally shaping into a cohesive *book* these individual poems has freed him to move into new areas.

Winter Journey has much to recommend it, not least its long title poem. There are poems which emerge out of myth and religious insight, poems of sensual and sexual awakening and loss, poems of wit and vision. They all share, as Barnes points out, "the recognition that significant junctures can never be securely fixed in mind or memory, together with the perception that one never arrives in Ithaca, so that apparent destinations turn out to be, with discouraging regularity, merely the threshholds to new wanderings. In the end . . . kinesis, process, is everything." Personally I don't find this prospect discouraging, and at least some of the time neither does Brown. Still, his tradition goes back through Roethke and Eliot, to Milton, to Horace even, and for some of those in it, to have to face that knowledge without faith in Christ would be more than discouraging.

The thing is, the poems seek to speak the unspeakable anyway; they focus on the ephemerality of grace yet capture something of the flavour of grace, however tentatively (as his consistent use of adverbs of possibility as adjectives implies). Also there are moments of comic lightness here, not least in the somewhat parodic homages to other poets.

In the title poem and elsewhere, Brown achieves a restless questioning of the very apprehensions which finally bespeak the world the poet (but not, usually, the poem) is unsure of. In "Canzona I," he gets at this paradox: "as the long day / repeating, divides / in brittle, the dim planes / of shape and shadow / . . . / our stillness becomes virgule / again the met gesture / of this word against word / unspeaking." The met gesture, whether despairing or desirous, is the figure all these poems seek to share. In their thickly consolidated syntax and continual refusal of easy answers, many of them achieve it.

In *The Blue Pools of Paradise* (Coteau Books, 1983) Mick Burrs reaches a new maturity in his poetry. Although the book achieves a mixed success, its general tenor, that of a delving into his family past, engages Burrs's heartfelt commitment in the best poems.

Burrs was born in California, of immigrant parents, and now, an immigrant himself, he imagines the lives and drives of his grandparents, and remembers his own past. One group of poems, including the title sequence, is pure memory. Although there are intriguing moments in these poems, and although they provide a genuine sense of immediate feeling, they also remain awkward and slightly out of focus. However, in the poems for his forebears, Burrs finds a sharper, more insistent voice, though even in these when he enters the poems himself, they lose some of their imaginative energy. Nevertheless, they stand as the best work Burrs has done. The search for roots has become a tradition in Canadian poetry, as Burrs acknowledges in his dedication of this book to Andrew Suknaski. In his best poems, he adds something real to this tradition.

George Eliot Clarke is a young Black writer from Nova Scotia, and his first collection, *Saltwater Spirituals and Deeper Blues* (Pottersfield Press, 1983), is a testament to and a celebration of his region and the history, especially the spiritual history, of his people there. Clarke himself notes the Bible, Hopkins and Dylan Thomas as influences, and indeed their presence can be felt in his poems; but there is also an earthy sensual joy that seems tied to the music he pays homage to in his title.

Clarke celebrates the past by writing poems in voices of that past; first in a series of poems titled after the various churches of Nova Scotia, and later in a poem sequence, "The Book of Jubilee," which celebrates the achievements of Richard Preston, who founded the African United Baptist Association. In between, he scatters poems of place, of love, of social commentary, some of which have real power and humour, some of which still display the awkwardnesses of a young, energetic, occasionally out of control word-monger.

Unlike so many poets today, Clarke enjoys the rhetorical flourish: sometimes his rococo alliterations are excessive, and sometimes his structures are too static. More often, however, he captures the flavour of spirituals and the blues in his verse, and the energy and music of the language carries the reader along. I enjoyed this book, on the whole; its youthful enthusiasm occasionally emerges as excess, but that's far more interesting than a tight little unearned cynicism. Clarke should grow and mature as a poet. This first book demonstrates he already has talent and energy.

Leonard Cohen never fails to surprise. Now the poet and songwriter who has scouted out so many territories of spirit and flesh has found his way into the terrifying and necessary territory of the soul addressing its gods. *Book of Mercy* (McClelland & Stewart, 1984), surely one of his most profound ventures, is a collection of what his publisher calls "contemporary psalms." There are fifty of them, rich in the rhythms and transformed images of the Bible, but rich also in the racy idioms and caustic wit Cohen has always displayed.

A courageous book? Yes. An outrageous book? Yes. A book of integrity? Yes. To write prayers today which are authentic and not the pious banalities of the moral majority requires courage, integrity, and talent. In these prose poems, steeped in the language of his multiple heritage as a Montreal Jew, we hear a voice committed to truth and fully aware that truth is painful, shocking, and mostly hidden. If it's outrageous, it is so in the service of vision, with recognition that absurd comedy is one of the means by which God teaches us.

Cohen speaks from the midst of contemporary pain and loss and doubt; his prayers are all the more real for that: "Though I don't believe, I come to you now, and I lift my doubt to your mercy." What fuels the doubt — *and* the desire for mercy — is shown with great black comical energy in #2:

> WHEN I LEFT THE KING I began to rehearse what I would say to the world: long rehearsals full of revisions, imaginary applause, humiliations, edicts of revenge. I grew swollen as I conspired with my ambition, I struggled, I expanded, and when my term was up, I gave birth to an ape. After some small inevitable misunderstanding, the ape turned on me. Limping, stumbling, I fled back to the swept courtyards of the king. "Where is your ape?" the king demanded. "Bring me your ape." The work is slow. The ape is old. He clowns behind his bars, imitating our hands in the dream. He winks at my official sense of urgency. What king, he wants to know. What courtyard? What highway?

But this is just one example, the mode of parable. In others, the speaker is more direct: "Bless the Lord, O my soul, who made you a singer in his holy house forever, who has given you a tongue like the wind, and a heart like the sea, who has journeyed you from generation to generation to this impeccable moment of sweet bewilderment." Cohen speaks as spiritual seeker: if he has learned that "From you alone to you alone . . . all that is not you is suffering, all that is not you is solitude rehearsing the arguments of loss," he also knows there is no single name by which to address "You." This is not orthodox Hebrew prayer. Cohen calls on "Our Lady of the Torah," a reflection of his continuing fascination with Catholic Maryolatry and the figure of the Great Goddess behind it. He provides examples of meditation that would be perfectly fitting to a Taoist or Zen Buddhist. He embraces all paths even if his keeps coming back to Jerusalem, albeit a city he sees as lost: "Jerusalem of blood / Jerusalem of amnesia / Jerusalem of idolatry / Jerusalem of Washington / Jerusalem of Moscow / Let the nations rejoice / Jerusalem has been destroyed." Still, as he insists, "Perceived or not, there is a Covenant beyond the constitution," and he will invoke it, again and again, for this generation.

Full of subtle changes, a great cry to the almighty made up of fables, instructions, tales, jokes, and always prayers, *Book of Mercy* is a book of startling purity of purpose and accomplishment. Cohen's language sings praises, even when he appears to be complaining. #50 is the perfect final prayer, a glory of affirmation in doubt and suffering. It closes the book; it opens the door:

I LOST MY WAY, I FORGOT to call on your name. The raw heart beat against the world, and the tears were for my lost victory. But you are here. You have always been here. The world is all forgetting, and the heart is a rage of directions, but your name unifies the heart, and the world is lifted into its place. Blessed is the one who waits in the traveller's heart for his turning.

Red Shoes in the Rain (Fiddlehead Poetry Books, 1984), the first book by Jan Conn, a doctoral candidate in entomology at The University of Toronto, ranges far and wide and engages all its various subjects with style and power. Conn has a scientist's eye, as the precision of her descriptions and meditations shows, yet the vision of the poet informs all her work with grace and intensity.

Red Shoes in the Rain is divided into four sections, and it's interesting to see how Conn has organized the poems in terms of their specific lyric qualities. Both "Choices" and "Japanese Journal" feature the lyric eye (I) of the poet as lover and traveller. "Cloudwhite paper" provides a good example of her method here:

> orange sunrise on grey water.
> fragments of ice clink together
> and pile on the frozen banks.
> a few ducks drift in desolate flocks.
>
> blue shadows cover the sundial.
> I cover my face. three snow geese
> fly west across the ruffled lake.
> I draw kenji in the silent sunroom
> overlooking grey patches of trees.
> scratch, scratch of black ink
> on cloud-white paper.
>
> downstairs, the clock chimes.
> echoes crowd the house;
> warm yellow memories of summer
> rise in the chilled rooms

But it's a poem of nostalgia for lost moments; many of the others question the loss of a lover. As do most of the poems from Japan, where the speaker notices the new beauties surrounding her but keeps insisting:

> I miss you. black hair & eyes
> ears curled like shells
> where waves pound and break
> on a ragged shore.

> is it accident or design
> that you aren't here?

In "The Rose Enters and Becomes You," Conn shifts into a third person narrative mode, telling sharp little tales of girls growing up and seeking escape into adulthood. The observation here is mordant but compassionate; the poems are fully aware of the almost sure possibilities of failure. "A Matter of Time," the final section, is more philosophical. There are some interesting attempts to make poems from novels like *The Wars*, but more interesting are the poems of psychological questing in the second person.

All in all, *Red Shoes in the Rain* is a remarkably assured debut. I feel that some of the poems aren't quite making full use of their potential notation — occasionally Conn breaks her lines awkwardly — but that's a small quibble when faced with such riches. If she can keep writing while pursuing her career in science, I feel sure she will be around for a long time. Hers is a gift to enjoy.

Dennis Cooley's *Fielding* (Thistledown Press, 1983), a long poem concerning his father's death, his response to it, and the renewed exploration of family roots and familiar routes in his home province of Saskatchewan, has been taking shape since 1980, when the first section appeared in *Leaving*, the poet's early chapbook. There is much to praise in *Fielding*, for it approaches and circles dark abysses of loss and pain with delicacy and discretion. Indeed, one of its subjects, and the root of much of the pain of loss it registers, is the silence the father practiced in his relations with his son, a silence which now can never be broken through.

Cooley's poem is full of silences, too, as he moves to apprehend his sense of loss with a tight-lipped understatement that applies to narrative and imagery equally. He recalls images of his father's younger days when the poet was a child, and images of the older man sickening and then hospitalized. He also recalls encounters with the rest of his family and with the landscape he grew up in, especially in winter, the only-too-appropriate time of his father's death. He also ironically interleaves examples of newspaper stories which ignore the private pain of ordinary people and letters of children which cannot recognize or understand the pain. Not everything works equally well, but the whole has a real power, especially the later dream of the "epilogue."

Cooley insists on a clipped poetic speech, yet it can be evocative, as in this passage asserting aspects of the past, the sickness, and the inheritance now alive in him no matter what:

> carbon phases / your phrases
>   strung between us father
> your breath tumbles
>   shining quiet
> inside my ribs

There must be something in the New Brunswick atmosphere, that so many poets from that region engage a kind of metaphysics everytime they encounter the natural world. Although very much a contemporary poet, Allan Cooper belongs to a line of poets stretching back to Carman and Roberts, and as his third book, *Bending the Branch* (Percheron Press, 1983), shows, he shares with them a sense of awe before the wondrous mysteries of earth.

Cooper's strength lies in the unassuming precision of his natural descriptions. Wandering around the wooded hill country of Albert County where he lives, on walks, fishing expeditions, and historical searches, the poet not only notices the natural life continually in process about him, but also sees deeper, further, into some spiritual core. Much of the time his transcendental vision leads him into a kind of egotism of the spirit; the poems, though keen in their insights, insist a bit too strongly on the privileged spirituality of the *I*. Nevertheless, as "Three Tiny Poems" demonstrates, he can beautifully connect microcosm and macrocosm via the interface of human awareness and language:

> Inside this leaf
> there are rooms of light
> where the chlorophyll swarms and sings.
> * * *
> I split open a maple log
> and find
> trees and a mountain in fog
> * * *
> IN LONG GRASS
>
> the place
> where a deer slept
> glows.

In a series of prose poems, Cooper becomes a supernaturalist/naturalist; the implicit Romanticism of his poetic stance is startlingly clear. And in the final section he traverses the fields of memory as well as of home to haul time's accretions into those of space. The book concludes with "The Final Gesture," dedicated to the memory of Alden Nowlan. Here Cooper gathers all his natural images into a large image of the soul's desire. A Romantic/transcendentalist gesture? Yes, but one grounded firmly in what the senses know to be present. The final section of the poem is both an expression of hope and a natural conclusion to everything the text has engaged throughout:

> We think that after death
> there is nothing . . . darkness . . . stillness . . .

> but perhaps we are moving at a tremendous speed,
> perhaps all our molecules are beginning to sing,
> perhaps their small ships are setting out
> in the final gesture
> of light

Not everyone today will find in the world the affirmations Cooper sees there, but there can be no doubt *Bending the Branch* offers a powerfully and generally strongly articulated version of its vision.

Jeni Couzyn's *Life by Drowning: Selected Poems* (House of Anansi, 1983) is a hefty collection in anyone's terms. All the well-known poems of this world traveller are here: "Christmas in Africa," "Inside Outside," the science fiction poems, "The Tarantula dance," "Karen Dreaming," and "Songs and Incantations," which were the centrepiece of her last book. There are some new poems as well, the most important of which appear in the title sequence, about the birth of her child.

Couzyn has a richly populated imagination, about equally fed by science fiction and the exotic flora and fauna of South Africa, where she grew up. They provide a wide range of analogies which populate most of her poems. It is also an imagination of violence, and although a sardonic humour leavens the violence in many of the poems, I was still surprised at how often it erupts into the poems. Love can act as an anodyne, but it often proves false, which heightens the pain. In the later poems, some of the "Songs and Incantations," some of the poems in the penultimate section, and the final, title sequence, love assumes a greater power, especially in the figure of the newborn babe.

Couzyn is a storyteller. Her poems tend to be narratives, and their narrators a wide variety of speakers. Her poems are an easy mixture of the contemporary and the traditional; there are even some dialogues of self and soul which Yeats would immediately recognize. The science fiction content of some poems allows her to explore the wider problem of alienation through a set convention of imagery which has its own poetic power, and aspects of that imagery then enter other, more 'ordinary' poems, lending them an aura of otherness both emotionally unsettling and intellectually provocative.

There are even some science fiction touches in "Life by Drowning," though there they appear in the early, philosophical sections, which are weakest. When she settles into simply describing her perceptions of her pregnancy and the joys of birth, she is more direct and emotionally evocative. This is a highly didactic poem in praise of motherhood, and it calls into question some of Couzyn's own earlier work in interesting ways. Whether or not readers find it occasionally overly sentimental will be, I suspect, a matter of taste.

Although few if any of the poems in *Life by Drowning* have any connection whatsoever with Canada, the book is an often forceful and absorbing work, full of energy and even didactic fervour. Though you may not always agree with her you will be impressed with Couzyn's imaginative power. There is much in it to praise.

As Lorna Uher, Lorna Crozier has published four books of poetry; *The Weather* (Coteau Books, 1983) is her first collection under her reclaimed family name and it contains some of her best work so far. Crozier finds, in the vegetation and animal life of her native prairie, images which speak her feelings; she enters this landscape and its inhabitants with a passionate apprehension and transfers her perceptions to us with powerful immediacy.

In the poems I find most attractive, Crozier discovers how to speak feelings through 'the other', be it owl, apple tree, or — in perhaps her finest poem sequence yet, "The First Woman" — the first white woman on the prairie. In many other poems, however, she fails to either transcend or transform the conventional lyric ego/eye, and the results sound like too many other poems by other poets. Interestingly, from my point of view, she tends to slip into more unnecessary similes in the more conventional lyric poems than in the poems where she is able to explore her own and others' feelings through the elements she apprehends so energetically.

Crozier's narrative ability comes to the fore in "Spring Storm, 1916," in which she reveals a fine capacity for deadpan comedy; in "The First Woman," which neatly dovetails Marie Lagimodiere's laconic tale of her life with the poet's search for a way to speak it true; and in "The Women Who Survive," another black comedy. Also notable are "Rooming House," where memory appears as distancing factor, and "Monologue: Prisoner Without a Name," which begins in cliché images but rises to a powerfully affirmative image of renewal at its end.

I still feel that Crozier could gain mightily from a bit more compression, especially if she'd push weak similes into tougher metaphors or drop them altogether. This is but a minor cavil, for *The Weather* is a strong collection on the whole and its leaves no doubt about the author's basic poetic power.

In *Edward and Patricia* (Coach House Press, 1984), Frank Davey reinvestigates some possibilities of traditional story telling in the long poem. As the back cover has it, this is a "rollicking poetic fiction," which seems an appropriate term for this series of fragments from a larger, more complex story. Why not write a short story or novella, then? I think Davey wishes to make use of a number of the conventions of open form poetry to distance and even interrogate the narrative of two young people falling in love, marrying, having the usual problems, and finally working them out or failing to do so. By telling this story in a series of dispassionately comic anti-lyric lyrics, Davey focuses our attention on *Edward and Patricia* as an essentially sexual tale; the poem as frame also allows him to ignore most other aspects of their lives except as they impinge on their sexual behaviour.

Set mostly in Vancouver in the 60's and 70's *Edward and Patricia* follows its two protagonists from college to early middle age. Patricia is a somewhat experienced experimenter who nevertheless leads an ordinary life, while Edward is a man with some cultural pretensions yet sexually naïve, aroused by Patricia partly because of her more wordly air concerning sex. The ups and downs of their emotional life together, as charted in their excitement or boredom with each other, makes for some sharply etched, acidly satiric, occasionally poignant vignettes from the marital front lines, and Davey achieves some especially fine comic effects with repetition and grammatical ambiguities at the line breaks.

Long poems have tended to assert their historical/mythical importance, their auto/biographical significance, or their serial imaginativeness. By telling a purely domestic tale, Davey recalls other possibilities (one is reminded somewhat of George Meredith's sonnet sequence, "Modern Love"). Although he is a bit too prosaic at times, Davey's wit and rhythmic touch carries *Edward and Patricia* forward to its suddenly bitter conclusion with authority. This poem deliberately refuses to be poetic in any of the usual senses, but by playing the conventions of domestic narrative against those of the long poem, it manages to raise intriguing questions about them both. Oh yes, it's also highly entertaining, sometimes outrageously funny, with moments few people will fail to recognize all too well.

Literary theorists have applied the metaphor of an archeological dig to the endeavour of both writer and reader in their confrontation with a text. In *What a city was* (Underwhich Editions, 1983), Brian Dedora applies the metaphor literally, offering us, in the prose fragments that make up this small book, the textual equivalent of pottery shards discovered in an archeological site.

The result is a collection of often sharply defined and perceptually precise articulations which are deliberately unfinished, fragments of a puzzle we will never find all the parts for. Because the city that these fragments (only partially) represent no longer exists, or perhaps never could have, they are referential in a most ambiguous manner. Pronouns float free of any nominal associations; what might in ordinary discourse be statements about people, things, or feelings also float free of didactic significance. Yet, because they are, even in their fragmentary nature, sharply articulated, often with a precision of image that insists upon response, something of the nature of this imaginative city takes shape for us.

What a city was avoids sentimental responses to loss and death, yet those are its central concerns. Reading these fragments is something like looking through a broken stained-glass window: what's there can only hint at what once was, yet the flashes of colour hint at the wonder people once knew whole. This is a difficult little book, but it offers strange rewards to those who engage it.

Born in 1921 and dead at the age of forty-nine, Éloi de Grandmont was a journalist, art critic, dramatist, teacher, and poet. He is not too well known outside Québec, but Daniel Sloate's generally sensitive translation of his poetry in *First Secrets and other Poems* (Guernica Editions, 1983) should go a long way towards changing that situation. This is a bilingual edition, allowing us to see and hear the originals. Still, for many of us, it's by the translations that we will know de Grandmont's vision. And although his first book, *Harlequin's Voyage*, is a poem sequence, he is essentially, and at his best both delicately and subtly, a lyric poet.

Harlequin's Voyage pays homage to surrealism in its shifting transformations of landscape into personality. These poems are intriguing in their way but they lack purity of perception. The poems of *The Girl Set in Stars* are a little less rhetorically flashy yet far more resonant in their imagery. Sloate says that de Grandmont's "own body of language is subtly erotic, infinitely delicate, beautifully restrained." This is certainly true of the finest of the lyrics in this section and in the later *First Secrets*, the very title of which points to the poignant pressure of remembered perception the poems display. "Sleep at Sixteen" is a poem of coolly analytical yet loving description. "The Awakening" is as translucent as what it celebrates:

> For hours now
> The sun has slept among your hair.
>
> Your body was swimming
> In the depths of the sea,
> Brushing against translucent fish
> And the shells of dream
>
> The calling waves
> Have put you down
> Upon a strand on fire
> Where now the day has you to watch.
>
> For hours now
> the sun has slept among your hair.

There are also two sequences in this final book, which manage, with an almost Yeatsian gaiety, to compel belief as the early surrealistic *Voyage* did not. "Farewell" creates a speaker/lover with whom we empathize in his love and loss. "Postcards" is an exquisite series of almost comic yet extraordinarily particular miniatures which suggest de Grandmont was discovering a whole new poetic when he died. Certainly he is a poet from our other culture well worth knowing, and Guernica Editions is to be congratulated for adding his work to its series of translations of Québecois poets.

In his second collection of poems, *Globe Doubts* (Quarry Press, 1983), Barry Dempster continues to display his faith that there is a social world out there and that it means something. His is a world observed by a humane and interested mind quite sure that signs and their referents maintain a close relationship.

This faith serves him best in his little social vignettes, careful observations of behaviour like "Mansion House: Men Only" or "Lakeshore Psychiatric" — the latter also one of his tightest poems. A sequence of poems on other artists and arts are not quite so focussed. Too often they read like the fragments of essays, and they lack precisely the curiosity — directed inward and outward through the play of language — which distinguished George Bowering's *Curious*. The later poems seem to be trying to explore problems of religious perception. They have good moments but finally fail to convince me.

Dempster is obviously serious about his craft, and his poems are competent compositions. He likes to use analogy and yet he continues to flatten the energy of his poetry with similes. There is a genuine psychological insight to his best poems, reflecting his experience as a psychologist, but there is also a kind of distancing in his poems which keeps this reader from becoming fully engaged with what he has to say.

Michael Dennis's pamphlet, *No saviour and no special grace* (South Western Ontario Poetry, 1983), is especially interesting for the manner by which the poet effects a distance between the narrative voice and the narrated figure in his tales of losers losing. "95 valium" is a good example:

> it's raining, saturday morning
> you wake up crying from the night before
> the kids came home late last night
> the kitchen is in a mess
> you're no longer sure about love
> yes love, that is the question
> you live with your husband of twenty years
> and you still have children at home
> the question is love
> what of it / where is it / where did it go
> you are trying to remember love
> the smell of it, the taste of it
> you want to remember the colour of love
> your eyes are circling the kitchen
> looking for the colour of love
> and it is nowhere to be found
> you contemplate the phone
> a black box of distant promise
> there is no love there
> the fridge, pure white

> a fat lady in a white sheet
> she is talking to you
> it is not a friendly conversation

Dennis catches the clipped tone of the pulps (which is likely what his protagonists would read if they read anything) but, alas, he also falls into the genre's characteristic trap of despairing sentimentalism on the next page where "you" is seduced by the fridge into a suicide attempt. But this second half of the poem should have remained unwritten, implicit but unsaid, for the last line of the excerpt is sharp yet full of implications. Dennis tends to have difficulty with his endings, going for what seem to be conventional gestures of despair.

Dennis's vignettes have bite, for he's a writer with a sharp eye for details. The problem with many of these pieces is that his syntax and line breaks all support a prose reading. The material captures our interest but there is little in the presentation to make us feel we are reading poetry beyond the fact that the right margin is uneven. Nevetheless, Dennis presents some compelling little tales of losers and youngsters who have not yet lost (but will, but will).

Certainly one of the most important books to appear in McClelland and Stewart's Modern Canadian Poets series, and possibly the most impressive single volume of 1983 is Christopher Dewdney's *Predators of the Adoration: Selected Poems, 1972-82* (McClelland & Stewart, 1983). Containing the first two volumes of his massive work-in-progress, *A Natural History of Southwestern Ontario*, and large extracts from *A Palaeozoic Geology of London, Ontario, Fovea Centralis*, and *Alter Sublime*, plus a glossary and an appreciative, helpful Afterword by Stan Dragland, *Predators of the Adoration* provides a superb introduction to the stunning mysteries of Dewdney's open, experimental imagination.

Dewdney's own charming Preface traces the early love affair with place and scientific exploration which infuses all his work. Its final paragraph provides the most important clue to the works which follow:

> In a sense, then, this book is the voice of the land and the creatures themselves, speaking from the inviolate fortress of a primaeval history uncorrupted by humans. It is a codex of the plants and animals whose technology is truly miraculous, and for whom I am merely a scribe.

As Dragland points out, this claim is not made out of false modesty: "He means what he says, and his writing supports him. There are 'voices' in it, but no single voice anchored in a lyric or narrative centre that draws the work to a univocal core of sound and sense."

Indeed, univocalism is the farthest thing from Dewdney's (receptive) mind(s). Since Dragland's Afterword deals so clearly and persuasively with Dewdney's philosophic stance and the ways it leads to "other voices," other universes of possibility, allowed into the interstices of his texts, I won't go into that here. The result is a breakdown of "normal" syntax, logic, and, indeed, *Weltanschauung,* all to demonstrate that the "normal" is something of a linguistic perceptual trap which poetry can break out of. Dewdney's own essays of explanation are both mind-boggling in their scientific-like arguments and hilarious in their skewed but finally possible rightness.

But the poetry, whether it be the anti-lyric mystery of such poems as "Transubstantiation" and "Grid Erectile" or the thickly imbedded meta-morphic prose of *Spring Trances in the Control Emerald Night* and *The Cenozoic Asylum,* is what counts. And it counts for a great deal. Not simply because he uses the languages of science with an authority few poets can lay claim to, but because for him all language has mysterious presence, Dewdney creates poems whose power resides in their intransigent immanence. The universe is multiplex, manifold, mysterious; the poems which engage its richly multifoliate being will be that way, too.

This makes for a difficult, opaque text, but not necessarily a forbidding one. As Dragland says, "a reader wants to keep loose, cultivate his taste for the unexpected." But then, as he adds, "it's good to read any poetry for its surprise, often finding irresolution even in seeming closure, rather than identifying what's familiar in it — to go with the magic, rather than trying to assimilate the poem to some more comfortable discourse." Dragland's point, and mine, is that there is great *magic* in Dewdney's poems; and the pleasure of engaging that magic openly can be great, too. That magic is present in such different poems as "Haiku" —

> My roof was once firm
> yet now it cannot even
> keep the stars out.

— and "Poem using lines spoken by Suzanne" —

> What you feel as your body
> is only a dream. The mind also
> is a slave. You are asleep.
> You are asleep, what you feel
> as your mind is only a dream. The
> dream also, is only a slave.
> You are a dream, what you feel
> as your slave is only a mind.
> The body also is a mind. You
> are asleep
> in the gentle theft of time. (time)

It is increasingly more powerfully realized in all its fragmentary and multivalent glory in the longer prose works. Dewdney's ongoing endeavour is a major contribution to the writing that counts in our time. It is definitely worth getting involved with, and the pleasures it offers, though perhaps hardly come by, are as real as the world(s) it encounters.

In the poem from which he takes the title of his first collection of poems, H.C. Dillow speaks of "This nominalist of the flesh, the seeing eye, / Content to live on orts and scantlings, scraps / From the world outside, and snippets of memory," all of which point to the fragments he measures out for us (in coffee spoons, like Eliot's Prufrock? perhaps, for the persona he often presents is at least as self-aware and bound by a spiritual propriety, and fearful of, if attracted to, sensuality — "the inevitable muck / of compulsive begetting" as he puts it in another poem — as Eliot's character was). *Orts and Scantlings* (Thistledown Press, 1984) is the work of a writer who has worked long and hard at his craft, and its poems are carefully made, imbued with intelligence and a wide range of literary and mythical allusions.

Indeed, Dillow, who was born in the Bronx and is now in his sixties, emerges as a modernist metaphysical poet, following in the footsteps of his beloved Donne, especially in such poems as "At a Solemn Wedding," where his dark puns insist that mortality be acknowledged even in the midst of the most lively art. His poems are thus arguments, often clothed in a richly symbolic language. They range widely, from poems of love lost and of love for children who must be lost for their own good, through poems of nostalgia for a thirties childhood of mythical figures caught up in the modern world, and of encounters with the philosophy of history, to a series of poems starring Bozo, an existentialist burlesque clown.

Dillow is fascinated by the "weather" of the mind, which he returns to in poem after poem, and which counts "as mere prelude to those major themes / Whose essence is more than leaves or stars fallen / To rot in earth and fund the life of things / That take their substance from such petty losses." That essence hovers about these poems, questioned, qualified, and querulously accepted in the end. Dillow's poetry seems curiously old fashioned, but with its air of learnedness it has its own kind of integrity. In its strict traditionalism, it stands out from much of the prairie poetry being published today.

Although it doesn't claim to be, David Donnell's *Settlements* (McClelland & Stewart, 1983) is something of a New and Selected Poems in that 32 of its 70 poems are revisions of poems from his previous two books. Having checked some of the revisions against their originals, I found them to be so altered they were essentially new variations on a common theme. In some cases, the changes may be slight, but in most, Donnell has created what are brand new poems; so I read *Settlements* as a new collection, and took pleasure in doing so, as did the judges for The Governor General's Award, obviously.

Donnell could be classed as a narrative poet, but if he is he creates stories more akin to the *Ficciones* of a Borges than to the anecdotes of a W.O. Mitchell (to point a contrast he humorously hints at in "The Canadian Prairies View of Literature"). "God expects you to produce a number of poems about opposites," he advises would-be writers in "How a Writer Should Explore the Nature of Fashion," and he seems to have heeded his own advice, for these poems are awash in contradictions and paradoxes, which they often flaunt with wicked comic precision. His poems are often small rhythmic essays, which reveal a philosophic mind mired in the body and its aesthetic encounter with the world. And though the voice of these poems is therefore that of a personal essayist, it is also the voice of the disestablished ego of contemporary life and art, unfixed, floating free in the ongoing changes of daily verbal commerce.

So although his title calls for a sense of place meant to provide a feeling of solid belonging, the poems argue an unsettled life, and the poet finds himself again and again, in the situation he describes in "Lakes," caught between the symbols of two different ways of life and unable to give up either. However, I don't want to give the impression that Donnell's poems are all heavy metaphysical meditations, though they often are like that; for they are full of satire and comic twists, and his control of sudden shifts of tone to astonish or delight is sure. He is one of the few poets writing right now who makes valid and exciting use of similes, as part of a developing argument in his poems. But that brings us back to the poem's essay-like quality. Although he does break his lines, they are long and quite prosy despite their often fragmented syntax. Sometimes they simply become prose, but usually he retains his balance and, in shifts of idiom and focus, insists on the essentially poetic nature of his enterprise.

Most of his poems defy quotation: they are too long to quote whole, and any excerpts would somehow miss the point. Their range is remarkable, from strangely universal dreams, through lists, meditations on artists and art, and a group of highly sensual love poems, to some terrifying confrontations with the darkness at the heart of human civilized endeavour. An example of the way his imagination reaches out from the immediate occasion to embrace the whole world is seen in one of his philosophical love poems, "Shoulders." Here is Donnell's poetic in a nutshell; the book awaits your further exploration:

> The strength of women's shoulders is a social reflex.
>
> Not the slightly bunched strength you see reaching
> for a box of papers on top of a semi-abandoned sea-captain
> bookcase
>   but the invisible strength with the resonance of a cello
> that you see supporting your body

in the evening light of bedrooms,

past the rapid scherzo of orgasm into the long minutes that follow,
      as if there is an effortless trick
by which our weight and momentum can be made to float
like a bruised swimmer with a torn mouth
who pauses at night on the calm waters the deep lake
inland from the violent coast
where the mud eel coughs our broken dreams.

Despite a number of awkwardnesses and too many typos, Meryl Duprey's *Tremen Town* (Gorse/Repository, 1983) earns one's attention. Duprey is writing out of the working and unemployed life of the Prince George region of British Columbia, so the poems contain a number of glancing descriptions of the rough and ugly lives of the young and old and middle-aged in such communities. Yet they are not realistic in any usual narrative sense.

Indeed, my problem with some of these poems is that I can't figure out how consciously Duprey may be attacking the conventions of realistic signification. Almost all the poems career wildly through tenses and persons, refusing to maintain a singular voice or the tale it might tell. The world of these poems is a shifty world of probabilities — most are bad, but some contain glimmers of hope or nostalgia, and none are fixed or permanent. This floating of the language so the reader can never quite pin down the referentiality of the words is effectively unsettling in many of the poems; in the rest it seems rather to be out of control and possibly just an example of syntactical dysfunction.

Still, given the power of some of the images and fragments of speech or thought in these poems, I have to say I think Duprey has found a forceful way to express the dysfunction of social order in the world the poetry engages. Rhythmically, many of these poems sound awkward to me, and the similes sometimes diffuse the force of the analogies, but on the whole this small collection argues well for Duprey's future as poet of a particular Canadian hell.

Claudio Durán is a Chilean-Canadian poet who now teaches philosophy at York University in Toronto; he writes in Spanish, and Rafael Barreto-Rivera has translated a selection of his poems in the handsome bilingual edition of *Mas Tarde Que Los Clientes Habitudes / All the Usual Clients Have Gone Home* (Underwhich Editions, 1982). Since I lack the Spanish I cannot speak of Durán's originals, except to say that the contents, as transported into English, reflect the great influence surrealism has had on South American literature and the philosophical conundrums Durán engages in his studies.

Barreto-Rivera's renderings are, as he admits in a Note, very free, but as a result they make for interesting English poems. Where the Spanish flows in long lines, he will offer the short, imagistic, lines of North American poetry, after Williams. The poems cover a lot of territory, from essence to being, illusion to reality, dream to nightmare. This is a small collection, but it nevertheless offers an illuminating glimpse of a poet whose vision is well worth sharing.

E.F. Dyck is a poet who likes to experiment and *The Mossbank Canon* (Turnstone Press, 1982) is, as he notes, "an experiment in form." Dyck uses the structure of the 64 *I Ching* hexagrams to shape his work and the connections of the musical form of the Canon to forge semantic and imagistic links throughout it. It tells the parallel stories of Mao Tse Tung and "Jong," a Chinese immigrant who ends up in Mossbank, Saskatchewan. Since Dyck has only 64 six-line stanzas to work with (and in my copy number 34 is only five lines), he is forced to compress and elide a great deal. Mao's story is present mostly by allusion while Jong's tale takes up most of the poem.

The Mossbank Canon is a fascinating though sometimes frustratingly opaque book. Having chosen the structure of the *I Ching*, Dyck also echoes its language and images; this gives the story a particular poetic resonance but also makes for a distant and uninvolved tone that leaves the reader unsure of how to approach aspects of the story. Jong becomes a pimp in Moose Jaw, and catches VD while Mao is beginning to fight the disease of capitalism in China. Are the ironies as powerful as they appear? Later Jong returns to China after being beaten by the Ku Klux Klan, yet his behavior to his wife is, by Western standards anyway, appalling. He returns to Canada and does well in some kind of deal with "the maharajah of Mossbank" while running the White Dove Cafe; meanwhile Mao leads the revolution. Perhaps it's Dyck's strategy to force us to make any moral insights these stories might allow when juxtaposed like this. Despite its austere distancing, the text appears to me to demand some such response, even while it also insists on not reaching any obvious conclusions.

So *The Mossbank Canon* teases us *into* thought through its formal play with what are rather ordinary stories. It is a carefully wrought work which maintains a certain distance from the reader yet insists that its reading be an act of engaged intelligence.

As if to prove that Dyck's not a serious boy all the time, the poet has also given us *Piss Cat Songs* (Brick Books, 1983), which is about as far from the cool austerities of *The Mossbank Canon* as you can get. These are raunchy barroom ballads as opposed to the classical restrained music of the previous book. As the "lady vet" says in "He lost his tanks," "Jack's a pissy cat," and these songs celebrate Jack as a kind of minor trickster, an agent of chaos invading the life and loves of the narrator. The puns and slyly undercut classical allusions of *Piss Cat Songs* signal a kind of carnival spirit. The owner may have Jack fixed and may *say* "I own him, body and soul," but the poems themselves argue a much more complex relationship in which the cat has certain powers to upset things which can never be wholly overruled.

These are anarchic melodies, raucous and energetic. Part of a larger work, they offer entertainment plus the promise that Dyck will continue to experiment with a wide variety of voices and viewpoints. I for one look forward to whatever he does next.

Margaret Dyment's first small book of poems, *I Didn't Get Used to it* (Ouroboros, 1983), announces its subject and its tone in the title. Here is a plain-spoken woman reflecting on her marriage, her children, the politics of being a thinking moral person in this country today. I like the person I sense standing behind these poems, but I'm not sure they're all successful as poems even when they succeed as commentary.

Dyment's verse is, like so many others' today, a loosely woven idiomatic speech, and usually her poems are addressed to a specific person: husband, lover (perhaps possibly the same person), daughter, son, the cop brutalizing her children at a peace demonstration. Her speakers speak plainly, refer to ordinary, often domestic, items as analogies. These poems articulate the concerns of a person most of us would enjoy knowing; but they are in no way unique, rather they fit a common contemporary pattern, and are standard examples of it. One will read this book, not for innovation or rhythmic power, but for the encounter with the personality who created it.

Mona Fertig's *Releasing the Spirit* (Colophon Books, 1982) is Colophon Chapbook Two, and it's a lovely production even before you begin to read the poems, with its Italian Old Face type, its Teton text paper, and its hand coloured illustration by the author.

The poems fall into two types: a short line, essentially didactic poem, often about the violence of the city, of war-mongering psychology, etc.; and a longer line poem full of unexpected periods, in which the metaphoric imagination soars and a powerful if gnomic sensibility makes itself felt. I prefer the latter, in which the poet discovers amid linguistic transformations images of the outer world which are informed by an awareness the conceptualizations of the other poems speak of but tend not to manifest concretely. The difference between the two kinds is that the first argues with us while the other convinces us emotionally. In the gnomic utterences a palpable mystery makes itself felt, yet it speaks of the world, in however transposed a manner:

> And there was fear the size of caves
> under my bed in the basement. The spirit
> or the intruder. The demon or the man.
> And small sparks of light I looked for
> to break their shadow backs. You have a
> will of your own. A tough rope to haul
> me in on. A master of subterranean

> thoughts. You drive the prayer through
> my plant. Unresolved you're a monster
> on my back. Child in the dark. The price
> of Imagination is its devouring danger.
> Then its spitting you out into the light.

In poems like "Child in the Dark," Fertig taps into an electric poetic force which does "release the spirit." Such poems make *Releasing the Spirit* a book definitely worth reading.

Hope's Half Life: Nuclear Poems by Raymond Filip (Véhicule Press, 1983) states its aims clearly from the beginning. The backcover puts the case succinctly: "This sequence of poems serves as a chronicle of conscience, an experiment in investigative verse. Real voices, real names, real places." And a real Preface by Gordon Edwards, National Chairman of the Canadian Coalition for Nuclear Responsibility, who says, "If we are going to survive on this planet, we will have to do it together. Appreciating each other's humanity is a good way to begin. These poems may help."

Well, yes they may, and I wish them luck, but I'm not so sure. The problem is that the people both the Coalition and Filip need to reach are unlikely to read this book; or to be moved by its arguments if they do. Filip ranges from hectoring chants (which could be fun in performance) to lengthy narratives of a protest march on Ottawa and a fact-finding visit to Chalk River. He does get to the point in the latter piece of showing Fred Blackstein as a good man firmly committed to nuclear power, but he is not convinced, and concludes, smiling "at the PR overkill. / Thank you but no. / Outside my window, / The glow of the snow lit up the darkness." Ok: Filip's stories and arguments are interesting, possibly even of immense importance to us all, but once again, I find myself recalling Yeats' words: "Out of the quarrels with others we make politics, out of the quarrels with ourselves we make poetry." I agree with Filip's politics but even so I feel these verses too seldom advance poetry, and it's poetry which might just possibly alter peoples' feelings and perceptions of the matter.

After not being heard from for sometime, Robert Finch has given us four collections of poetry since he turned eighty, the most recent of which is *The Grand Duke of Moscow's Favourite Solo* (Porcupine's Quill, 1983). Like the others, it is full of witty, often subtle and basically humane light verse. I choose that term advisedly, yet it seems to me to be the correct one. Finch plays intelligent and comic variations on a number of traditional forms; he writes with clarity, elegance, and verve; yet even in the most serious poems of the fourth section, poems rooted in his Christian faith, he refuses passion or indeed any profound emotion, seeking instead to entertain us by entertaining ideas and images in a light and gentlemanly manner.

There is much to be said for such a refusal of the grandiose. Indeed, though the whole first section is "about" the favourite flute solo of a Grand Duke of Moscow, it is more a collection of tales and lessons concerning music and art, and is most an extended and graceful compliment to a friend, the Sue who plays the flute and who appears to be one of the dedicatees of the book. Such graceful gentlemanly literary gifts belong to another age, so it is all the more refreshing to find someone still able and wishing to practice the craft of making them. Perhaps this is Finch's most important gift to readers of the 1980's.

One reads this collection, then, grateful for the humane conviviality of the verse, for its pointed and intellectual wit, for the traditional qualities of craft it manifests, not to be swept away by its power. Finch is an Age of Reason Classicist, not a Romantic. Still, there is much here to be grateful for, not least the vision of a gentler, more stately way of life these verses celebrate in their fine formality.

"Pure outrage will keep us alive / attentive, though we continue to suffer it," says Cathy Ford in *By Violent Means* (blewointment press, 1983), and if the outrage fuels her imagination in these poems, it does not overwhelm the attentiveness she brings to her materials and the language with which she articulates what she perceives. As the title suggests, these are poems born in anger, in desperation, but also in love and compassion. The book is dedicated to many sister artists by name but also to "the gentle men too," and the poems tend also to be directed to particular people so we read over the intended reader's shoulder, so to speak, sharing an intimate speech pregnant with possible meanings.

Ford works the language hard here. Lots of gerunds and participles, lots of periods miming the continually frozen gestures of the heart seeking freedom, lots of free floating parts of speech as the poem surges with barely controlled emotion. In some of her earlier books I felt she hadn't completely maintained the necessary control over her lines, but here the opaqueness of some of her syntax is a precise rendering of emotional complexities too exactingly dissolved under pressure to be expressed any other way. Or sometimes too gently subtle to survive prosaic descriptions, so only the metaphoric analogues of poetry can net them.

I don't want to give the impression that all is anger here. In the second half of the book Ford also celebrates friendship and love, as well as the survival that allows both to be. She refuses to close her eyes to human pain, and her work is deliberately, almost violently, political in its insistence on seeing what is wrong in the world, be it in interpersonal relations or in international ones. Tyranny, whether sexual or social, is her target. Yet she also notes the beauties that are still to be found, and she desires them with an erotic intensity. This is a powerful book.

Bill Furey's editor, David Solway, has done him a signal service by putting "Resurrection Song" first in *Night Letters* (Véhicule Press, 1983), for this savagely comic and toughly compassionate poem demonstrates Furey's poetic vision in an almost perfect articulation:

> Get those skeletons into tuxedos
> for the resurrection party, boys
> get those flesh coats on them.
> Crown those skulls, slip in those eyes,
> stitch on those arms and thighs,
> pin on those virginal genitals,
> insert those ribs, that heart,
> patch up those bullet hole bones,
> smooth on that hair, those lips, those hips.
> replace those gassed lungs, those famished guts;
> put wind in their eyes,
> tear off those cloths of odorous gauze
> and paint their faces with beautiful infant smiles.
>
> "Come out you headless patriots
> you victims of the guillotine
> replace those severed limbs and parts,
> you suicides of gas and rope
> rendered corpse by beam and oven;
> all you who deserted in the face of cannon.
> out of your soldier coffins;
> and you martyrs, rise up and come forth."
>
> Shut up carcass, mercy will work this out.
>
> Break that lock on the trunk of flesh dresses, gang,
> carry out those new hands and legs,
> those sparkling membranes;
> like newlyweds under the bridge of bridesmaids' arms
> the dead run back into the world again.
>
> Bring them back to the love stalls
> in their new carnal gowns,
> breaking like roses from the January clay
> and rattling with sensuous joy
> their redeemed and happy sides.

Without that one line stanza, this is a good, rough-house poem. With it, it approaches transcendence and yet without losing any of its crass materialist vitality. This poem grabbed me and led me into the rest of the book with pleasurable anticipation.

On the whole, Furey delivers on the promise of "Resurrection Song" in *Night Letters*, though nothing quite comes up to that performance. An ex-Newfoundlander now living in Montreal, Furey appears to have picked up many of the literary influences in his adopted city. Some of his lyrics owe much to Leonard Cohen and his personal poems have something in common with his editors, Solway and Michael Harris. He is, nonetheless, very much his own man, especially in the way he deploys his sardonic but not unsympathetic humour across his poems. I find he is best in poems which borrow their voices from other texts, like "Ballad from Villon," or in poems where he slips the demands of the Romantic I by addressing a "you" or a "he" who floats free of the usual lyric signification. Some of the love lyrics, while well-wrought, sound too much like others' lyrics, especially the young Cohen's. He also slips into conventional weak similes a bit too often, though his metaphors can be exact and penetrating.

Notwithstanding such carping, *Night Letters* is a highly entertaining, complex, and often compelling collection. We'll be hearing more from Furey, for he is capable of a powerfully ironic poetic speech. Meanwhile, this book invites us to share a quirky and lively imaginative vision.

Lost Language: Selected Poems by Maxine Gadd (Coach House Press, 1982), edited by Daphne Marlatt and Ingrid Klassen, collects a large sampling of work from 1958 to 1980 by this elusive poet. Although Gadd has published only three small chapbooks, gathered together as *Westerns* in 1975, those who have heard her perform over the years knew she had a huge corpus of work to draw on. This collection provides an overview of Gadd's poetic career from her late teen-age activity in downtown Vancouver's art scene to her present retreat on Galiano Island.

Although Gadd is her own person, it might help to compare her, in terms of philosophy and approach, with poets like bill bissett; and like bissett she is a powerful performer of her own work. Reading her, we quickly discover that hers is a poetry of possessed voice(s): the lines use the whole page as field, the spelling is of the moment and liable to change (though not in any way so metamorphic as bissett's), and syntax is shattered in the drive for pure vocalization.

The editors have divided the poems into three sections: "City and Wilderness (1958-1967)," "The Hippies of Kitsilano (1967-1971)," and "Islands (1971-1980)." As they point out, "this is the work of a poet with a marvelous density of voice." Or perhaps that should be "voices," especially in the poems of the second decade. Although one can fairly safely identify the main voice of the early poems with the figure of the poet — and a very Romantic, not to say Rimbaudian, figure that is — there is often no main voice in the later poems but only a conjunction of voices both high and low. In an intriguing interview with the editors, Gadd points to both her early encounters with public rhetoric and her later encounters with goddess speech as groundings for the flights of voice her poems enact.

Not all the poems will work for any reader. Sometimes the various voices fail to come clear. Sometimes there's a kind of syntactical or superficially hippie interference. But the best works have immense power in their savage juxtapositions of vocabularies and social idioms. Some of the recent poems achieve a kind of transparency of content which utterly foregrounds the speech act that has always been central to Gadd's art. This can be seen even in one of the few short poems, "The hunter," where the voices may stick to the point, but they come at it from every point of the compass:

> the hunter walks in the sun, the hunter misses
> the sun. whoever made sorrow yr lover? visit the sands of
> Egypt. don't
> step into Cinderella's shoes. get yr sweet boy on the road
> on the sea, be as free of him as the hunter
> is of the deer.

Gadd trusts that "sacred," and when she does allow it voice, purely, things really happen in her poems. Then the rush and swoop, the flight of the tongue, can be felt, in the score of her poems on the page.

In dedicating her first book to Denise Levertov, Susan Glickman shows great taste in choosing poetic mentors, yet not all the poems in *Complicity* (Véhicule Press, 1983) demonstrate that she has truly learned that poet's implicit lessons on open form composition. Indeed some of Glickman's poems seem awkwardly prosaic and unsure of how to achieve a viable notation. Others, however, especially her stunning "The Physics of Desire," suggest that she can annotate the subtle movements of thought and speech in a manner that would surely please her dedicatee.

Glickman has divided *Complicity* in three parts. In "From the Balcony," she tends to deal with family and social life. The best poems here are "The Country of Old People" and "Going Home," where she develops a real feeling for the often unrealized need to belong to a genetic history. "Oranges" is a three part meditation on gifts of nature, and points toward the darker celebrations at the end of the book. "Cold Days" contains poems about love in various contexts. Some contain witty lines yet seem to fizzle into vagueness or the expected. "The Physics of Desire" explodes into its centre, powerfully evocative of feeling whetting the intellect till both feeling and intellect are almost too sharp to bear. "Naming the Dragons" is also successful. The poems in the title section, including the poem of that name, suggest another aspect of Levertov's work, its commitment to social and political change. Their power is possibly dependent on the reader's agreement with their political stances, but I found "Complicity" itself undeniably moving. And the final two poems, "Grace" and "After Such Pleasure," in their celebration of the joys of friendship after the darkness shown in earlier poems, present a hopeful sign at the end.

Complicity is an interesting first book by a writer whose intelligence and basic humaneness are clearly present in all her poems. Despite some awkwardnesses of form and tone, the book as a whole augurs well for her future endeavours in her craft.

North Bound: Poems Selected and New (Thistledown Press, 1984) is a perfect title for Leona Gom's latest book, for as this exemplary selection demonstrates, her strongest poetry has always been bound and bonded to the Peace River country in Northern Alberta where she grew up. The winnowing process which has produced this volume has managed to exclude almost all the weak and cute poems from Gom's previous three books. The result is a collection whose integrity of vision and memory is utterly grounded in the experiences of childhood and youth in a harsh farming country which insisted on "connecting forever / the knowledge / with the guilt" of understanding.

Gom is one of the plainest spoken poets we have; there are no experiments with form or language here. There is illumination, however, hard won and informed with the clarity that only escape and nostalgic return can bring. Gom offers views of herself as the youngster growing up and seeking to escape the farm to the city, but more important are the subtle psychological portraits she offers of her parents and of some of the other denizens of the community, especially the women. Gom is a powerfully moral writer, and her angry sympathy is what makes many of these poems work, for, as someone who strove long and hard to become an outsider to the demands of that place, she knows just what kind of strength and desire people had to have to survive there. She still bitterly resents the easy denigration of city folk, and she has erected these poems as a monument to celebrate the terrible and wonderful "battle" (more glorious than 'real' war, as one of her poetic ancestors, Isabella Valeney Crawford, argued in her settler's epic a century ago) her people fought in order to tame an inhospitable land.

North Bound is the best introduction to Gom's work so far that one could hope to find, for it contains the strongest of her poems, which are, as she has admitted in "These Poems," the ones which "keep crawling out / from under my pen / and running back / to the north. / They will not be domesticated." Yet, as the "New Poems" here suggest, she has just about pumped the well of memory dry. The recent poems bring her up almost to the present, even to making a return all these years later to find no one remembers her. It strikes me that *North Bound* is Gom's deliberate attempt to write finis to her explorations of the origins of her art in that stony, unforgiving ground. Simple, plainspoken, these poems have a force and integrity based on their open-eyed acceptance of what was. After the pleasures of reading this book, however, I, for one, am left intrigued by the question of where she will go from here.

Leroy Gorman has been called "one of the most talented young poets lighting up the Canadian haiku scene," and his latest collection, *Heart's Garden* (Guernica Editions, 1983) goes a long way toward substantiating that claim. North American haiku is a peculiar form; like its Japanese predecessor, it proves that small is beautiful, but it still lacks a history of profoundly meaningful conventional figures (although, with such a wide spread interest evinced in magazines and anthologies, it's possible a vocabulary of tropes is being slowly built up). Individual haiku can be powerful but when a whole gathering is put in front of a reader, something more is needed, some larger form of organization.

Gorman has attempted to create the needed sense of structure in *Heart's Garden*, organizing his poems into five sections, "Neither Here," "Into Place," "Two Daughters," "A Farm on the Rideau," and "A Home in Napanee." The power of his best poems — in which he proves that even smaller is even more beautiful — is dissipated in the ongoing rush of another impression, and then another. For example, in the section titled "Two Daughters," he is forced to repeat the title phrase, or its equivalent, in almost every passage (the haiku were probably originally published in many different places), but since we read the whole section as a single piece, the repetition grates.

There are haiku here, however, which show Gorman exploring the boundaries of the form, especially some delightful, near-concrete pieces. And, as an example of the beautifully tiny, here is one of the finest pieces in the book:

> shade
> cicada(')s
> call

Gorman hasn't convinced me that a book of haiku works completely, but he comes closer to doing so than many others have done. I still think he will someday have to find a way to build larger structures out of his often stunning aperçus.

Elizabeth Gourlay prefaces the two sequences which make up *The M Poems* (Fiddlehead Poetry Books, 1983) with this explanatory note: "M / / stands in the middle of the / alphabet // Moon Memory Mother." The twenty-nine poems of Part I are all about the moon, while the twenty-three poems of Part II concern the poet's mother and her influence. Memory plays an equal though different role in both sequences, for in Part I it functions mostly as historical/mythical memory while in Part II it's the poet's personal memories which feed the imagination.

Part I is intriguing in its mix of scientific speculation turned to imagery, factual quotations, mythic interpretations, and personal feelings. One can sympathize with the poet's desire to engage all the modes of address to the moon which humanity has practiced through the ages, but some of the individual pieces are too dry and prosaic. The effect of the whole, however, is of an historical collage, a bringing into the one textual space fragments of texts from many layers of past imaginings.

Part II is much more homey and direct: here the poet speaks of remembered scenes, remembered tales of her mother's remembered life. If "in the long run / existence is ordinary / humdrum / nothing lives up to / the romantic dream," Gourlay at least offers us some clearly articulated scenes of that ordinary existence which meant so much to her; and by doing so, she gives it a touch of the vibrant life it had for her.

Although *The M Poems* is a small book, of limited ambitions, it breathes a spirit of humane recollection — of the personal and mythic inheritance we all share on some level. It won't overwhelm you but in its unassuming way, it will touch your feelings.

It is, I suspect, especially difficult for a North American poet to create a valid and meaningful explicitly political literature. Pablo Neruda's example is a great one but we do not live in his context, a context in which both the need for a political statement and the large audience willing to listen to it existed. What is the concerned writer to do, then? Dennis Gruending has confronted this problem head-on in his first book, *Gringo: Poems and Journals from Latin America* (Coteau Books, 1983), and he has succeeded in overcoming the difficulties more often than not.

One reason for his success, although it occasionally leads him into a somewhat pretentious egotism, is his decision to mix journal entries and poems. Gruending is a professional reporter, and much of this material demands a reporter's cool, detailing eye rather than any kind of poet's frenzy (especially as his poetry is also fairly straight-forward — the only two viable possibilities here, it would seem, are reportage or a crazy surrealism, and the latter seems to be the exclusive property of the South American writers themselves).

I agree with Gruending's political stands in this book, but his assertion of these is not what's important. What's important are the notes on ordinary people whom he meets, and on his sometimes frightening experiences with the representatives of power in such countries as Guatemala and El Salvador. What's important are the images of natural beauty and human compassion which fill the poems. There's also the occasional flash of satiric bitter comedy, as in the poems on Pinochet, a buffoon who can murder too many.

Gruending's journal entries on his affairs and on his personal thoughts about writing seem out of place. His eye sees most clearly and most sharply when it's directed outward into the alien spaces he passes through. Most of the time he does his job, documenting one man's learning *in* the places he seeks to comprehend. As a result, *Gringo* is an evocative book which seldom falls prey to the terrible temptation to preach. On the whole, it artfully avoids becoming mere propaganda, and as a result it achieves a real power to touch us all with its truths.

Although he has long been praised for the intellectual wit and cultured urbanity of his poetry, Ralph Gustafson has not always received recognition for the lyrical emotions he has consistently evoked through a career of close to fifty years. *The Moment Is All: Selected Poems 1944-83* (McClelland & Stewart, 1983) is a perfect title to sum up Gustafson's life-long obsession. Although clearly a modernist rather than a post-modernist poet, Gustafson has always celebrated the evanescent Now, even when one aspect of living in the Now is paying attention to the art (artifacts) that represents all the Nows, now lost in Then.

Only a third of his present collection is made up of material which appeared in Gustafson's 1972 *Selected Poems*, and that alone speaks volumes about his increasingly prolific output as the years have passed. Yet what is truly interesting is to see how similar, formally, the early and late poems are. Gustafson developed very early the staccato, constantly shifting syntax which in his poetry signals a mind active and accumulating arguments for feelings which continually batter the soul's gates.

Don Coles, who made this selection, has wisely kept the whole of the "Rocky Mountain Poems" (including four new additions to the sequence). It remains one of Gustafson's finest accomplishments, wherein the massive Canadian land, awesome as brute fact, engages and delights while conquering the mind soaked in European culture. The poet's precise rendering of that engagement points to the witty and wise observations of daily life which fill the recent poetry. The poet acknowledges Nature's raw power, but continues to insist on Art's civilizing function. As he says in one of the "New Poems": "What man creates in meaning is / The world we live in though the rocky / Earth is what we ride on." *The Moment Is All* is the work of a poet who has never tired of celebrating that ride, though he has never flinched from exploring its dark moments as well as its bright and glorious ones.

The centrepiece of Phil Hall's *A Minor Operation* (blewointment press, 1983) is the long title poem, a series of meditations on past and present possibilities occasioned by the poet's vasectomy. Accompanied by analytical drawings of the operation itself, the poem searches through memories and dreams for signs of valid manhood in a complex world where love includes acceptance of the loved woman as a whole person, and where masculine failure to make that acceptance can still be read as "real manhood" (as in the portraits of the father-as-hunter). The poem is witty, tough, and psychologically acute in its sudden shifts of focus.

The other, shorter, poems in *A Minor Operation* are directly or indirectly connected to its concerns. Hall is consciously striving to overcome the sexism he grew up with. Both the operation and the poems it engendered are parts of his attempt to search out the roots of this sexism in his own familiar past. So there are poems about his mother and father as well as poems about his failures with past lovers, his attempts to destroy his early self, and his attempts at genuine love now. "Javex," for example, is a savagely comic poem of self-hatred in a child; it also shows the poet's technique:

> I drank myself
> to death
> as a boy
>
> never spat
> on the sidewalk
> and swore
>
> I drank myself
> to find the Javex
> in time
>
> I swallowed
> the Javex
> in time to feel desire
> enlarge me
> in my parents' eyes
>
> I don't know why
> the past was so tense
> in their eyes
>
> or why I drank it
>
> Childish I guess
>
> You could make
> so many things
> out of Javex bottles
> then
>
> I wanted to make
> something
> of myself
>
> I wanted the past
> pumped out of me

A Minor Operation is both interesting in itself and as a sign of Phil Hall's continuing development as a poet.

In *The Black Bird* (Porcupine's Quill, 1982), David Halliday uses *The Maltese Falcon* as a means to focus on the questions of fame, illusion and reality, life and death, memory and fiction, as they might affect Humphrey Bogart were he an existentialist philosopher rather than simply an actor whose cinematic iconicity brought out the existentialist philosopher in many of his viewers and, it appears, in Halliday himself. And though there are moments of brilliance in the book, there is too much that seems out of focus, perhaps because Halliday has tried to do too much — tell a story of Bogart and also a psychological history of the modern world.

The Black Bird contains excerpts from Bogart's "diary," which shift around too much in tone and allusion; a series of "Newsreel" poems, which attempt to tie world events into the making of the famous film *noir*; poems in the voices of both the characters and the actors who played them; and a posthumous "interview" with Bogart. Like some kind of stylistic virus, the pulp writers' overuse of similes practically takes over the book. Occasionally the similes are marvelously hard bitten and fitting, but more often they are unnecessary. The "diaries" are too self-consciously literary to be believed, though on the whole the "interview" does work, perhaps because it's so obviously fantasy we accept its intellectual overreaching.

This book will prove interesting, if also somewhat disappointing, to fans of Bogart, Hammett, and *The Maltese Falcon*, but will probably prove only confusing to readers who don't know its base texts. Halliday can write powerfully, but here he's tried to make one analogy carry too much historical and intellectual weight. The book sags under its pretension, despite some lively and engaging moments.

Elizabeth Harper's father was a Baptist minister; her mother a music teacher: their combined influences can be felt throughout Harper's second book, *Octaves of Narcissus* (Fiddlehead Poetry Books, 1984). Indeed, the title poem holds up the God-forsaking city against its early self, where people gathered in harmony. Narcissus, too self-aware for his own good, is the image of forsaking this poet argues against throughout the carefully structured analogies of these poems.

Harper sees signs in both the natural and man-made world around her: she reads scripture in ploughed fields and grass lands, hears sermons when "The decent woman drinks." Sometimes, her vision of the ordinary reminds me of Margaret Avison's, but she seldom achieves Avison's grace of rhythm and language. I must confess, nevertheless, that I enjoyed most those poems in which she neglected to make an obvious point. The imagism of "Japanese still life," and sections of the sequence "Sea Structures" engage the world as presence, sufficient unto spirit in and of itself, and that moves me more than moralizing can.

Harper expresses fine and sincerely felt sentiments: "There was a world / before 'and', / before that first of our / compassionate conjunctions." She is even capable of humour in faith, as "Mercy" shows: "How kind is God the Father / . . . Son-of-a-gun! . . . / and God the ghostly Mother / handing out assurance at the bar." But I keep waiting for these poems to take wing and they simply don't. I listen respectfully but I am seldom *moved* to assent to their vision.

In *Out from Under* (Oasis Publications, 1984), his fourth book, Rolf Harvey is especially interesting for the way he handles narrative. The very first poem, "Dreamscape," offers clues to his method. He is willing to evoke traditional images of story, but he couches them in a telling which quickly shifts away from the traditional to the nightmarishly contemporary. The world of these poems is our world, but it is our world refracted through the paranoia of the modern thriller, and so even the possible pastoral of a visit to a grandmother's farm takes on the aura of fear that so often hovers over Harvey's poems.

Many of these poems, and for me the best ones, tell their tale in a bare bones language stripped of rhetorical flourish and, if they must trope at all, do so with the most concise and naked metaphors. Midway through the book, some of the poems become more ornate, and a number of similes lacking punch appear. Most of the poems do not lack punch, however, for whether he speaks as contemporary poet aware of the attacks on writers and freedom-fighters in various countries, as a child confronting human cruelty, as an ancient pharaoh, or as an aging lover, Harvey offers pithy visions of the world as terrible arena. Yet, if when he watches army manoeuvres, he caustically comments, "the stupidest men in the world / sneaking around out in the rain / with guns and serious eyes," he insists on adding, "We had to wipe / the mist from the windshield / in order to see it clearly." In that insistence on seeing clearly, Harvey claims our attention, and in describing what he sees without overstating or fuzzing it, he maintains it. *Out from Under* is a tough little book.

Robert Hawkes is a native of a small town in New Brunswick, and the spiritual ambience of such a background plus a boyhood in the Depression and the War makes itself felt in nearly all the poems in *Paradigms* (Fiddlehead Poetry Books, 1983), his sixth collection. Hawkes is primarily a narrative poet, telling low-key short stories of loss and entrapment. Here his subjects range from the death of a child to incontinent old men in a nursing home, touching the bases of youthful fantasies of escape and historical examples of puritan repression along the way.

Hawkes's poetry is plain-spoken and direct; there is a dryness and hint of the kind of wit associated with New England, which isn't surprising when one reads a poem like "Ironics," with its specific references to the Loyalists. In the tale poems, Hawkes sets his incidents out in as few words as possible; in shorter idea poems, he says exactly what he thinks. "Assimilation" provides a good example of his technique: "Some say / we are / the sea // the losers / but a drop / of dye."

Hawkes approaches cynicism but is saved from it by genuine compassion for the figures in his best poems. These show us a way of life, often constricting but allowing insights, which occasionally his speakers realize. *Paradigms* is a quiet book, but at its best it has a real power.

"I've always wanted to get it right / but it's not a question / of getting it right," says Brian Henderson in his brilliant new series of poems, *Migration of Light* (General Publishing, 1983). It is the unspeakable that migrates, and although we often know it intimately we know it only on the move, where it can't be pinned down in words, despite the fact that it is in the fields of language we discover traces of its passing. So Henderson keeps trying to get it right, even though he knows that "now there is no script at all."

"Whatever is simultaneous / it is not love or language," yet these are the twin foci of Henderson's explorations in *Migration of Light*, as he wanders in reflections, aware that "we have to lose something in order to see," and that "Whatever is, I guess you could say / whatever we see / keeps pointing onwards into the blackness / which almost welcomes us / without a single backward glance." Light fragments everything, and it is always in motion: how fix emotion then, in words? Henderson isn't sure, for recognizing both "the white / amnesia of snow" and "the white / amnesia of sex," he is left with the loss of words which are all we have, finally, to speak our knowledge: "Trying to live / with this: like writing / by the perished light of stars / The result is illegible."

Henderson's triumph is that he has produced poems which are not illegible, though they are complex. They are also precise in their imagery and imaginative in their spiritual explorations of the erotic life of nature and art. The "First Migration" is made up of separate poems which query the possibilities of writing out of such experiences at all. Even as they almost deny it can be done, they tentatively manage to do something. The "Second Migration" is a sequence of memory. It's in the "Third Migration" and its first four "series" that Henderson discovers a poetry of immensely powerful positive denials. Sex and suicide, the tension of perceptual feeling, the fragmentary articulation of how "this moment" of connection or disconnection impinges on the senses — again and again, Henderson finds the words and rhythms to invoke experience. It is in the "Series" of the "Third Migration" that the book truly sings, but the whole is dependent upon all its parts, for the idea of "light" and what it can signify grows and alters throughout the book. And Henderson knows that every time the "light" changes, all he wishes it to illuminate does, too. "What happens among the stars / happens among / the finished light we still see // It's the shining makes it clear / so that everything remains the same / and is not." Heraclitus knew this light, as well. Henderson's poems articulate mystery by allowing it to remain mystery — clearly seen, and outlined in the poems, but beyond analysis, finally simply there to be said (to be seen) as sharply as possible. Here's the final poem, and the book does lead up to it, necessarily:

The metaphor, if really lived, derealizes
the world, and only the metaphor
is real. The metaphor holds the earth
back, holds it, and itself, fares forward
with an almost absolute sense
of wonder
        and also nostalgia
as of the still living lives of
the dead in us, those
we have left behind forever

Forever
who gather
us

the way the sun, going under, gathers
all colour to itself
and gives it to the sky

Migration of Light confirms Henderson's status as one of the most exciting poets to appear in the 70's and one who will add considerably to our literature in the 80's.

Robert Hilles's first two books revealed a young poet who seemed to recognize some of the problems in poetics a self-aware writer faces today. Sometimes awkward, they nevertheless manifested his conscious struggle with the terms of his craft. In *An Angel in the Works* (Oolichan Books, 1983), two Hilleses are present: one is a lyric poet often locked in traditional poses; the other is more the poet-as-experimenter, attempting once again to find a new and integrated speech.

Part One, "This Sudden Emotion," is a product of the former figure. It seems to me that a major difficulty with the love lyric today is how to free it of convention, of conventional responses (which are fine if you're in the mood, but which sign a poetic stasis for the writer who truly seeks to "make it new"). Some of the individual lines in these poems are delicately inspired, but the poems as a group figure the romantic lover/writer in all his self-centered appraisal of the other. And that figure, the privileged I/ eye singing his love, is conventional.

Part Two, the title sequence, is much more interesting. Something of an homage to Jack Spicer, it floats the signs of its speakers so they cannot be pinned down to any one figure, though sometimes the speakers are lovers, poets, and others. Part of its fascination lies in its questioning of language and its powers. As well, there is a heady impression of improvisation throughout, as the poem wrestles with the very concepts to which it owes its being.

Part Three, "The Black and White Word," is another collection of lyrics; although not as wholly inscribed by conventions as the poems in Part One, these represent something of a comedown from "An Angel in the Works." Nevertheless, poems like "The Black and White Word" push outward, refusing the temptations of egocentricity the conventional lyric seems to offer today. On the basis of this his third collection, Hilles remains a poet to watch yet he must watch out for himself if he is not to slip into conventional poses in his poems. Because he has shown he can aspire to something beyond the conventional, and because, in poems like the title sequence, he continues to push at the boundaries of his craft, I think we'll see more exciting work from him soon.

"I was going to write," the first poem in Gary Hyland's *Street of Dreams* (Coteau Books, 1984), holds up the usual epic dreams of elsewhere — Cole Younger, Sam Lord, and others — only to say that his poems will come from personal experience and memory:

> But every time I spun
> their sheets into my machine
> surprises emerged
> runny-nosed Home Street kids
> afraid of Binner's snapping dog
> Sleight Hill shoot-outs
> piracies on Thunder Creek
>
> Whenever I went for Cole Younger
> my arm was grabbed and jammed
> between my shoulder blades
> by a grinning Nazi Miller
> the best clarinetist on Home Street

Or so it seems. Like Hyland's last book, *Just off Main, Street of Dreams* mainly concerns itself with anecdotes of growing up in a small prairie town, including some sharp character sketches of youthful companions and various adults the narrator encountered in his youth. From poems of almost pure imagism to rhyming light verse, Hyland covers a lot of ground, in terms of both form and content. Sometimes the rhymes are a little too cute (as in, say, the voice portrait of "Mr. Kroski"), and occasionally memory trips into undiluted nostalgia. As well, a series of poems which self-consciously deal with the problems of writing poems fail for me because of a Romantic sentimentality.

Many of these poems, however, make clear why one reviewer said Hyland's last book was "required reading for those who insist contemporary poetry is boring, unreadable, esoteric." Although I don't agree with that reviewer's implicit condemnation of so much contemporary poetry, there's no denying that Hyland's sense of the comic, his ability to coolly demonstrate the appalling emotional cruelty kids are capable of, and even his sometimes mawkish portraits of smalltown losers have an immediacy that reaches readers. It's partly due to his anecdotal approach to the poem, but when it works it results in highly readable work. Hyland is especially good at catching the speech of his characters. "According to Crazy Dave," for example, both demonstrates that skill and shows that the writer is fully aware of what he's doing in these poems:

> He was always kinda hard to swallow, eh?
> Y'know, a liar. Like if he said somethin
> you never really knew if it happened
> or he saw it in some goddamned movie
> or just thought it up in his bloody head.
> Like when we played guns, he'd make up
> these stories or plots or whatever
> that were so krisely far-out we'd waste
> more time listenin than playin.
> Another thing, he spent a lot of time
> alone by himself, eh? Just walking around
> or sitting down along the creek there
> or up in that old loft in his back yard
> so that's probably when mosta this crud
> more than likely really happened —
> like not at all if you know what I mean.
> Let's face it, eh, I was there as much as him
> and I never seen halfa this crapola.
> I mean it's nice he's got a book and all,
> but as far as I'm concerned it's mostly shit.

Street of Dreams is an entertaining addition to the growing shelf of books about growing up on the prairies, whether or not Crazy Dave is correct in his critique.

Frances Itani's second book of poems, *Rentee Bay: Poems from the Bay of Quinte (1785-89)* (Quarry Press, 1983), is essentially a poem for voices, and I can envisage it as an historical radio play. Its main characters are Emma and Mark, a Loyalist couple, their servant Bett, and the children. It follows their settlement on the Bay of Quinte until the so-called "Hungry Year," when a winter of extreme scarcity almost finishes them.

Itani allows each speaker mainly pithy and concise speeches. The context of her poems is documentary, although the characters and their story are fictional. And though she uses natural tropes to carry part of her argument and to foreshadow the disaster to come, this is essentially a realistic tale. Basically, then, the poem works as an understated study of early settlement in Canada; there is nothing flashy about it, but the cumulative effect is real and moving.

Reading Karl Young's fascinating essay on "Notation and the Art of Reading" in *Open Letter*, 5:7 (Spring 1984) has prompted me to look at all poetry with my eyes more attuned to its various possibilities than before. A case in point is the work of Beth Jankola, specifically *Sun/flowers* (blewointment press, 1981). Typed out, much of Jankola's writing seems flat, but bill bissett has reproduced her calligraphy and drawings, juxtaposing them in various ways, and the result is page after page which, however awkwardly sometimes, invites us to slow down and trace the words and images with aesthetic care.

No doubt Jankola lacks the subtle mastery of the Chinese scribes Young speaks of; nevertheless, her calligraphy, sometimes light and tiny, sometimes heavy and thick, and sliding between these extremes, signifies the mood in which the writing occurred. Since these tiny jottings take on a mind and heart in process, akin to haiku in their delicate immediacy if not in their subtlety, their appearance as handwritten gestures is wholly appropriate. Jankola's drawings, all variations on the sunflower icon, are a curious mixture of the naïve and complex. The large forms are almost too simple, yet the actually calligraphic filling in of the forms signals concentration and complex effort. Again the message relates to the act of making the art rather than to some "deeper" theme. Jankola leads her life, observing the people around her with compassionate humour, and she distills her observations into quick written takes which she then surrounds with natural icons of femininity. The result repays a reader's contemplation if approached in the proper receptive mood.

Report, Process, Evidence, Productions, Intimations, Definition, Appreciation, Composition, Relationship, Ambition, Content, Environment, Abstractions, Transmigration, Mediation, Meditation, Involvement, Explanation, Death, History Lesson, Domesticity, Expression, Projections: these are some of the titles from Lionel Kearn's *Ignoring the Bomb: New and Selected Poems* (Oolichan Books, 1982). They point to an aspect of his work which has remained prominent throughout his career. His editors suggest that he "is one of those rare poets who has realized that words not only are, they also say," by which they mean to point to a quality of valid referentiality which many writers no longer fully trust. And George Bowering has pointed out that "most of his work combines two interests that are not often seen together: leftist humanism, and comedy." And Kearns, in one of his best known pieces, "Manitowan Poems," lays it on the line:

> I want to tell them this
> that you must struggle against your fear
> You must press that feeling out of yourself
> and make it into something hard and real
> a picture or a play or a poem, because
> outside it turns into something else:
> energy or information or love

> the forms and flowers and things
> that someone, somewhere, sometime
> will come upon and learn and know
> how you felt to be alive. That is
> poetry, and has nothing to do with
> fame or applause or approval
> Poetry is the struggle to be in this world
> yourself in spite of everything
> It is the struggle of life against death
> of the hero against overwhelming odds
> and it is everyone's struggle
> > because we are all heroes

This struggle is at the core of Kearns's work, and it informs it with compassion as well as comic insight.

Most of the titles I listed to begin with are abstractions. Abstractions figure prominently in the vocabulary of teachers, and Kearns is clearly a didactic poet, though a subtle and often duplicitous one. But what is interesting about those abstract titles are the poems attached to them: they are usually highly concrete in image and event, and so in emotion as well. Kearns is writing poetry, and though be believes "a successful poem can remind us that some acts are still less absurd than others" (which is to say that the creative and imaginative act of *Ignoring the Bomb* is what poetry is all about), he also writes with considerable craft. This is a warmly humane as well as an angrily satiric book, and one which will provoke thought as well as laughter and delight. Readers who have not yet acquainted themselves with Kearns's poetry should wait no longer.

Although Don Kerr's *Going Places* (Coteau Books, 1983) is as much a travel journal as it is a poetry collection, he is a good fellow to travel with. Kerr has a fine sense of humour and humanity. His pleasures are the small ones we all understand: the cold beer at the end of a long day's drive; talking with friends found once again when they live scattered across this vast land; the visions of prairie, mountains, and sea scape.

Going Places moves from Kerr's home of Saskatoon across the prairies to Calgary, through the mountains to Vancouver and Vancouver Island (with a side trip to San Francisco), back to Edmonton and finally home again. Most of the travel is by car, his wife driving, but in fact the poems hint that a number of different trips served to feed the imagination that finally produced these poems. Most are anecdotal, the thoughts and impressions of a good man wide awake to his surroundings and keen to articulate the passed or passing scene.

Kerr tells a good story, for he knows enough to laugh at his own pretensions. Some of his insights sparkle: shopping, he says to his wife, we "received for our paper / a dress so splendid / we thought it must belong / to somebody else / and looked at it sideways / afraid it might

53

disappear. / So now you are someone else." The plainspokenness of this text is representative; it offers its own small but solid pleasures. And in a few poems, like "Old Men at Stanley Park," he digs a bit deeper, hits a gnomic chord and offers a glimpse of primal mystery. Most of the time, however, we hear Don Kerr, a fellow we'd enjoy listening to over a beer. He can be depended on to have something interesting to tell us and to make us smile at how he says it. Although lacking the rhythmic subtleties I associate with poetry at its best, *Going Places* offers entertaining anecdotes with satiric bite.

The Sharpshooter (Sidereal Press, 1983) is Ronald Kurt's first small collection, and in it he wisely sticks to something known and felt: his father's experience as a youthful draftee in Russia with the German Army and his own ambiguous relationship to that past in a country where battle is styled in a Hollywood studio. The poems are small vignettes, and in their intense appraisal of behaviour they are sharply etched miniature tales. This is good insofar as they are tales, memories to be retold, but it also leads to a somewhat prosaic presentation. Nevertheless, the gritty realism in the presentation is worthy in itself.

Slowly the process goes forward; and with every new Selected Poems from Irving Layton we are given a better book. Thus *A Wild Peculiar Joy* (McClelland & Stewart, 1982), co-edited by Layton and Dennis Lee, with input from Wynne Francis, Eli Mandel, and Seymour Mayne, is, at approximately 150 poems for the whole period 1945-1982, a vast improvement on the over 275 poems in the two volumes of 1975. On the other hand, over a third of the poems are from the last six years, and I would have to say that's too high a percentage. Layton can rave that Neruda lacks a shit-detector, but in terms of poetics he seems to be without, as well.

It can be seen that I don't feel a great need to discuss the poems themselves. Well, it's my considered opinion that any person who follows poetry in Canada today and does not know Layton's work and what it represents must be eccentric, indeed. What can be safely said is that *A Wild Peculiar Joy* is the best book by which to introduce Layton to a new reader. And some of the most recent poems have a purity of vision I could wish appeared more often. There are some ironies for the longtime Layton reader, too: the poem for his daughter is a miniature of Yeats's more famous and greater "Prayer for My Daughter," but Layton has another poem in this selection (let alone some of his introductions) attacking the elder poet. And his savage misogymy still overwhelms the famous *joie de vivre* and love of women he boasts of: there are some very ugly poems attacking women here, like "Everything in the Universe has its Place" (1982).

Layton remains a figure to contend with. He is inescapable, no matter what one thinks of him. This new Selected has many virtues, and will be definitive — until the next one.

Meanwhile, *The Gucci Bag* (McClelland & Stewart 1983) reminds us why Selected Laytons are so necessary, at least to readers. Layton undoubtedly needs the freedom of a whole new book to fill every year or so to grant him the room to practice his craft at a continuing high pressure, but of the results of all this activity — 105 poems in this collection, for example — only a few will pass the test of time. Certainly the misogyny and misanthropy take their insistent place in *The Gucci Bag*; the poet has lost a lover/wife and in his pain he lashes out at everyone. Of course, in his Foreword, he chooses Jack The Ripper as a metaphor for the Times to explain the bitter anger that informs so many of these poems, but the poems speak of more personal origins (and although he may not know it, other writers have already found Jack a fitting figure of our troubling and terrorized age).

Layton's essential conservatism of form, his conventional lyricism, gets stronger as he gets older. There are a few shapely images of the natural world as it greets the poet's eye with joy; there are lengthy lectures addressed to such other poet/fools as Pasternak; there are the customary lyrics celebrating the lusty young bodies of new women; and there are the poems of bitter hatred addressed to the cheating women and men who have betrayed the poet or his ideas. The sincerity of these poems is not in question but the power of their craft and language often is. Layton tells us how he feels more often than he shows us. As has so often been the case with Layton collections over the past ten years or so, *The Gucci Bag* contains some powerful poems, but the diligent reader will have to search for them. The Layton fan will no doubt love the whole bloody bird.

The poems in Ross Leckie's first book, *A Slow Light* (Véhicule Press 1983), get progressively better as the collection proceeds. I note that some of his work has appeared in the *Vancouver Surrealist Newsletter* and find that most of his shorter poems display all the qualities I find irritating in third or fourth generation surrealism. They are slick and facile, they make all the right moves, they *feel* empty.

The poem sequence, "The Caroling Breakers," is a refreshing step out of glitz and into something more substantial. The voice of these poems seems to be grappling with the world and it does so with a certain wit but also with some genuine feeling. When Leckie writes, "the words! the words cower in shame / and inadequacy, that cannot tell of their love, / or have told it so many times / they can no longer be heard," one feels his genuine desire to seek a way to speak a commitment to the world out there.

Intriguingly, it is by using other peoples' words that Leckie best expresses that desire. "Correspondences" is a group of poems "made up of words, phrases, images, and lines taken from various authors' journals and letters, spliced together with some of my own notions." It is as a warped and wry scholar and editor of others' speech that Leckie most fully finds an idiom of integrity and these pieces are the most engaging in the book. For them, especially, is it worth investigating.

Wise and witty and also very small, the minimal gestures of Lola Lemire Tostevin's *Gyno Text* (Underwhich Editions, 1983) ask us to pay careful attention to the creative movement through time which they chart with such subtlety (I am reminded of bp Nichol in Book IV of *The Martyrology*, being told that with "such minimal movements to seek truth in" he will be "accused of shallowness" and responding with the thought that that would be "hallowness feminized"). Sacred and profane are always close to each other in these poems, and when they touch they are often brought together by a pun.

Paring language and rhythm down to the barest fragments of inherited structure yet allowing each word its full connotative play, Lemire Tostevin seeks to slow us down enough that we may enter with her the process whereby the "becoming of subject is affirmed and developed." That the subject in question is both children and the possibility of art is, she tells us in her Afterword, what she has discovered in the writings of such feminist theorists as Adrienne Rich and Julia Kristeva (who uses the terms *pheno-texte* and *geno-texte* for familiar as opposed to generative language use). The poet explores the roots of generation in herself and finds a double birthing of children and poems: *Gyno Text*.

In English and French, Lemire Tostevin creates her delicate nodes of language, each small poem a lovely element of linguistic meditation demanding our alert response, yet also part of the larger structure of the book which is transformative and an articulation of process. The delight one feels when reading at the beginning

> V
> notch
> of I
> dentity
>
> a
> legend
> at
> leg's
> end

increases as we watch the legend grow and take shape throughout the poem until the final words:

> *vagin*
> *vagir*
> *enfin*

A small book, *Gyno Text* is a seed that grows if the reader enters it in the right receptive mood. Only Lemire Tostevin's second book, it nevertheless signals the continuing maturation of a remarkable talent. She is writing new, and she is doing it well.

Something Still to Find (McClelland & Stewart, 1982) is Douglas LePan's first collection of poems in almost 30 years. These new poems cover a wide range of themes and forms, but they all seem of a piece with "A Country Without a Mythology" and "The Net and the Sword," poems of over three decades ago. That is not a negative evaluation, merely a descriptive comment which also argues the consistency of LePan's poetic.

Although the poems in *Something Still to Find* range from mythic narratives to personal reminiscences, from love songs to meditations, from animal tales to elegies, from satires to philosophic inquiries, they share a language I can only describe as Romantic laced with modern slang. The stance is essentially Romantic, too, especially in poems like "Red Rock Light," a study of isolation in nature leading to possible transcendence; "A Radiance," an elegy which seeks the same kind of consolation as Wordsworth's "Ode" and Shelley's "Adonais" did; or "A Rough Sweet Land," a long meditation on the Canadian land as place wherein a mythic figure might grow. These are among my favorite poems here because in them LePan's strenuous rhetoric finds themes which can uphold the high-flown language he brings to bear.

Some of the short poems, with their sharply defined images and symbols, are also arresting. In "Lessons of the Hummingbird," LePan begins by philosophically engaging the subject: "It suggests we could have our own kind of ecstacy / if we would." He then turns to consider its uniqueness to the new world, shifting to a description of its evanescent beauty — "this tiny heart that keeps the wings so furiously beating / Till time stands still, in a transparency, / a clot of deeper light on the sunlight over the rock / rose trellised on a stem of air" — then to a further meditation on what we can make it signify, and then, further, to a short sentence of simple acceptance and celebration of its pure being. The accomplishment of this short poem is large, is greater, in fact, than that of many of the more extensive and obviously learned poems which have perhaps a bit too much of the odour of the study on them.

Still, LePan is a subtle craftsman of the old school, and a writer who has gained much wisdom in a long life of service to the language and its literature. *Something Still to Find* lives up to its title in its best poems, which offer a sense of the possibilities life still holds out to us.

Douglas Lochead's *The Panic Field* (Fiddlehead Poetry Books, 1984) contains the long title sequence, an 18 poem sequence, "In A Winter Apartment," which he says is a love-poem, and a group of individual prose poems. It is a book of undeniable power, even if, at times, the focus seems a bit unclear.

"The Panic Field" is based on pocket-diary entries kept by the young Lochead when he was in the Army during WWII. Over the years, the poet has added to and revised the original entries, but he has maintained the flavour of the originals throughout. The work is a sly piece of memoir-making, and as is the case with all memoirs, it is impossible to tell where fact leaves off and fiction begins. At least, Lochead has made his central character, the young officer-in-training who knows his vocation is to be a poet and who romantically queries all that is happening to him in terms of how it will affect that vocation, an authentically comic figure. Which is not to say that the horrors of the army — especially the endless training for a battle he never saw (at least in the poem) — aren't clearly articulated. They are. And the narrator's care for his fellows is genuine. On the whole, "The Panic Field" offers a cool vision of a hot and hotly apprehended time in a young Romantic's life.

Although "In A Winter Apartment" is called a love poem, it is a poem full of anger, some of the same anger that first found tongue in the Army. Perhaps the lover addressed is the muse in part. For many of its sections express failure, frustration at not finding the right words or, if finding them, finding that they "pour themselves into heavy lead." Here is *13*:

> I live into myself, it is the black
> road around boulders. now is the time
> of telling. I listen and the answer
> lies frozen. the ice is a green depth.
> clear but telling nothing. nothing

Tart. Abrupt. Possibly despairing. But not completely, since the poems emerge, even if they "are what I take into / my damnation" trying to tell something else besides "the ways / of God" which "are straight and told."

The shorter poems are a mixture of domestic and pastoral lyrics of acceptance and slyly savage satires by a leading scholar in Canadian Studies of the ways Canadian Culture has gone astray. They bring to a close an altogether sardonic book. It is interesting for its continual refusal, in all its varied pieces, of the traditional lyric stance, one which Lochead's other books have tended to take. All in all, *The Panic Field* offers some uncomfortable but compelling views. It is a significant addition to Lochead's previous work.

To all lovers of the absurd and paradoxical I have no hesitation in recommending Steve McCaffery's *Knowledge Never Knew* (Véhicule Press, 1983), a stimulating and jarring performance masquerading as a book. It is in fact a carefully structured series of irruptions meant to call in question the key concepts of writing, reading, book, and anyone's relation to all three. The sainted shade of Jacques Derrida hovers over the proceedings (and he is very much alive, as we all know, don't we). Most of the book is white space, cleverly devised for us to fill in or at least to fall through, from distorted "history" written above to sadistically seductive mind-bending aphorisms (what McCaffery, the back cover tells us, "terms condensed ruins") below.

"are the words you read / the same as the words you see?" / can be taken as a useful example of McCaffery's methodical madness here. Consider. Perhaps you'll consider further. Keep considering, but note, "the writer writes / the reader writes upon the writer's writing / the writer reads." McCaffery finds the proper aphoristic tone; he sticks to it, *and* he sticks it to us. I find his little pieces stimulating, funny, and genuinely poetic in their disruptive power of thought. Not everyone will like this book, but I think it's both provocative and delightful.

Jerome McCarthy, an Anglican priest born in Ireland, now lives in Southwestern Ontario. These and other facts of his life inform the poems in his first small pamphlet, *Eden & Other Reservations* (South Western Ontario Poetry, 1983). "On Leaving Ireland 1978" and a few other poems have an Irish lilt to them, the language fulsome and melodic in a traditional manner. McCarthy's vocation has perhaps a greater influence on his writing than even his homeland, however: most of these poems are arguments from and to faith in which the things of this world — daisies, ships in the Welland Canal, a young prostitute, lilies, snakes, even ICBMs — act as signs of the larger Text he wants us to read.

I enjoyed some of these poems. McCarthy writes of Ireland and her sectarian struggles with a sane passion, and his sympathy for the underdogs, including that prostitute, is genuine. "Passover," a gruesome pun on the missiles bringing Armageddon, is also a triumphant vision of faith fulfilled. It's an awkward, frightening poem. Nevertheless, his urge to teach tends to turn his poems into homilies. They read as logical arguments where analogies and images exist only to serve the development of the point. The priest tends to command the poet, and though that is probably proper from the spiritual perspective, it does not always make for the most inspired verse, however inspired are the feelings and insights which impel it.

In last year's *Chronicle* I praised Don McKay's *Lightning Ball Bait*, and here I am this year adding to those praises my recommendations of his *Birding, or Desire* (McClelland & Stewart, 1983), a book which covers a lot of territory yet never strays far from home. McKay's is a continuously metaphoric imagination and, armed with his trusty *The Birds of Canada* plus his knowledge of family, friends, and the landscape around London, Ontario, he effects multiple transformations on our quotidian reality. It helps that he also has a wicked sense of humour.

As the title suggests, McKay is a birdwatcher and he finds that activity and the writing of poetry have much in common. More to the point, however, he finds in birds and their behaviour analogues for much else he wants to talk about: "On the other / hand a swallow's evening has been usefully compared / to a book comprised entirely of errata slips. // He wings it."

This, from the first poem, points the direction these poems will take and suggests something of the improvisatory and exploratory feel they have.

What they also have, time and time again, is a precision of perception and response which is exhilarating, especially when, as in the best poems, it is delicately scored in the notation. McKay both knows and loves his birds, which is why he can see them clearly for what they are, as in "But Nature has her darker side, " "Swallowings," or "Kestrels," to name just three. But it's his very respect for them as they are that allows him to see further, to see them imaging other possibilities, in our complex human lives. Because his imagination encounters them in such a rich profusion of allusive connections, he is able to create similes (usually in a series) which surprise and delight and do not usually strike the reader as metaphors manqué. The birds must be allowed their separate place, and the people theirs, yet they can be compared. Sometimes he invokes the analogy with such subtlety we hardly notice it's happening; at others, he interrogates it in order to pull the world, and us, its readers, back into clear focus, as in "'The bellies of fallen breathing sparrows'" (which will remind us of one of Leonard Cohen's most famous lyrics, if not of many others):

> Some things can't be praised enough, among them
> breasts and birds
> who have cohabited so long in metaphor
> most folks think of them as married.
> Not only that, but
> when you slide your shirt (the striped one) off
> the inside of my head is lined with down
> like a Blackburnian warbler's nest,
> the exterior of which is often rough and twiggy
> in appearance.
> And as the shirt snags, hesitates, and then
> lets go, I know exactly why he warbles as he does,
> which is zip zip zip zip zeee
>   chickety chickety chickety chick.
> The man who wrote "twin alabaster mounds"
> should have spent more time outdoors
> instead of browsing in that musty old museum where
> he pissed away his youth

This is one of McKay's least rambunctious poems, but it offers a nice sampling of his methods. *Birding, or Desire* contains some sharply realized images of natural life but it also contains some brilliant snapshots of domestic life in process (I think "Smash the window," about his daughter's thirteenth birthday, is a wonderfully humane and compassionately comic poem). My only complaint is that 25 poems are also in *Lightning Ball Bait* and though McKay offers an explanation, that's still quite a few poems from a book still in print. Notwithstanding which, I recommend getting them both. McKay is worth it.

Susan McMaster, Andrew McClure, and Claude Dupuis are members of First Draft, an artists' group in Ottawa, and these three, a poet, a musician, and a visual artist, have collaboratively developed their own form of performance poetry, the texts and notation for which appear in *Pass This Way Again* (Underwhich Editions, 1983). It is a book to intrigue and delight anyone interested in the concept of performance poetry, for it makes it clear that they have created a viable and rich example of the form.

Pass This Way Again is a collaborative project, just like their performances. Claude Dupuis' illustrations, simple in basic design yet complex in their patterning, perfectly reflect the sounding systems they accompany. Susan McMaster's poems shift from the traditionally lyric through the chant-like to the gnomic. After their appearance as straight text, Andrew McClure's performance-notation frees them into an imagined largeness the potential listener can satisfy herself with until she can hear the artists 'play' them.

In every case the notation for (usually three) voices both extends the oral possibilities of the original poem and frees its language from conventional signification. This can be seen most clearly in such conventional lyrics as "Alberta fall," a poem I suspect is one of McMaster's earliest pieces. "Scrapbook," which is a list of things and actions, signals its debt to the process it is intended to enter, and is far more intriguing both as pure text and as score. But the whole book glows with intelligence and the collaborative spirit; I heartily recommend it to all readers *and listeners* with adventure in their souls.

Susan McMaster also has a small pamphlet out: *Seven Poems* (Ouroboros, 1983). The poems in it are more straightforwardly narrative than the most adventurous pieces in *Pass This Way Again*. Idiomatic, they render the sharply perceptive speech of an observant mother, lover, friend. There is humour and compassion here but there is a certain prosaic rhythmic looseness at times too. I kept wanting a greater tightness in some of these poems, metaphors toughing it out where similes now loll. But I enjoyed the person the poems presented, and figure the poet can and will get better.

Prefaced by a line from Robert Frost — "Call it a day, I wish they might have said" — but taking account of all the possibilities in the phrase, *Call It A Day* (blewointment press, 1984) is Eugene McNamara's work-poem collection. In it he has culled poems from previous collections and other publications to create a general collage of impressions of the workplace. Luckily for us, McNamara's usual wit and sharp perception are at work throughout, so the book is genuinely entertaining in its anecdotes of a (usually young) man's encounters with the frustrations and ironies of "the job."

There are two longer sequences in *Call It A Day*. "Punching In" is the more interesting of the two because its narrative voice is obviously related to the young McNamara, and the embarrassments, successes, games, and general hard talk recorded therein strike the reader as honestly presented, however sexist, silly, or savage it may be. "In the Plant" is an attempt to tell a life-story through terse notations from one limited perspective. The concept is more interesting than its execution. The other shorter poems render aspects of the working life with irony, compassion, and occasional nostalgia.

This is very much a book of masculine vision, and in that fact lies its fundamental honesty. This is what life in the factories used to be like and McNamara records it with an apparently innocent eye and ear. But, in fact, his control of language and rhythm slides a filter of awareness over the whole scene. This is a small book but it can move its various readers to nostalgia, to anger, and to laughter.

On the cover of Daphne Marlatt's *How Hug A Stone* (Turnstone Press, 1983) is a hand-tinted photograph of some of the stones at Avebury. The act of recreation implicit in the hand-tinting — the artist's imagination *going over* what is simply perceived and providing a patina of *vision* — that act radically grounds Marlatt's thickly textured writing in this poetic journal of a journey back to origins. And Marlatt is only too aware that the Indo-European root of "stone" is "stei," which means "to thicken." She erects her own henge of words rooted in the fields of language to the memory of her late mother in *How Hug A Stone* by imaginatively recreating the moments of recovery the journey evoked.

In 1981, Marlatt took her 12 year old son, Kit, with her on a visit to the England and the family she had not seen since she was 9 years old. As usual her prose poems register every nuance of perception and response as she encounters places and people for the first time in thirty years. As well, partly by registering his responses in her own articulations and partly by quoting him, she allows her son's new encounters with ancestral ghosts to become part of the complex palimpsest she is creating. Indeed, she weaves a web of various voices, all impinging on her consciousness and through it on her text. Thus she avoids the temptations of mere gossip or confession by continually discovering in the language of the place what it has to tell her of her past and present.

The narrative *is* personal as it records her encounters with relatives, including her 90 year old grandmother who speaks from a time and culture now lost, her fluctuations of fear and remorse as her son suffers allergies and boredom, her desperation as she seeks to discover the mother who never spoke wholly to her in life. But "narrative is a strategy for survival": Marlatt's story as it happens has all the cumulative detail that a precise rendering of the continual present can carry. Miming her active, thoughtful, emotional perceptions, her complex syntax is terribly honest in its consistent refusal of the consolations of convention. If there is difficulty, then that, precisely, is the poetry. Reading, one realizes with exhilaration that one is sharing the awareness of a delicately tuned, highly charged, precision instrument of articulate perception. And because the encounters *How Hug*

A Stone registers are as often with people as with places, a humane and always curious humour plays across the text, balancing the fear, rooted in the failures of her mother's relationship with her, that she will similarly fail — as a mother who still feels too close to her own childhood — her child. Indeed, forms of "the mother" abound in the book, leading to the ultimate figure of such power, the Great Goddess, who is felt in the stones at Avebury, which return the poet to the womb of language. Out of that confrontation emerges an acceptance which can even confront and live with the political horrors of the present.

Through imagination, through dream and fever, through the love that is there in families, the poet comes to the point of return. A warm, humane, loving, sometimes comic, sometimes frightening, always exhilarating book, *How Hug A Stone* involves us in one of the most basic of all quests, and at the most basic level — the language by which we can tell who we are.

Solstice (South Western Ontario Poetry, 1983) is Cathy Matyas's first collection and it reveals a young poet of potential. Matyas has a naturally metaphoric imagination, and she continually divines metamorphic signs in the natural world around her. Her poems betray their apprentice nature in their failure to achieve concise phrasing, in her general tendency to use a weak simile where the stronger metaphor would have more force.

One almost imagist poem, "The Couch, the Ear," is a lovely rhythmic sketch.

> Pink con-
> cavities whorled
> organs   fluted
> lobs   mimetic
> echoes of seas
>   auricular
> ear against ear
> and drumming
> of waves

It doesn't try to do too much but it does catch one's attention. In other poems, Matyas attempts more, trying to connect perception to its implications, investigating the emotions of a particular event. I find the person implicit in these poems interesting and worth knowing, but I also want her to sharpen her focus. What's good about these poems suggests she will get better. Meanwhile *Solstice* offers us a glimpse of a talented poet still learning her craft.

Although all of *A Bride In Three Acts* (Guernica Editions, 1983) is fueled by an intense anger, the book fails to hold my interest as much as did Mary Melfi's last book, *A Queen Is Holding A Mummified Cat*. In one of these bitter essays on the state of married life (I call them essays because their rhetoric and rhythm is deliberately prosaic and argumentative, though not lacking in punch), Melfi creates a character named "Rage, the bride, with a bicycle chain around her neck." In fact rage is omnipresent in these pieces, railing in overwhelming frustration at the way things are. As the book moves through its three sections — in order: "Act Three, Scene Four," "Act Two, Scene One & Two," "Act One, Scene One" — the reader expects a passage backward in time which creates structural ironies to parallel the sarcasm of the individual sections. Such a movement almost occurs a few times in the final section, but all the pieces are so alike in tone and mood, one doesn't read much alteration in the whole.

There are lists, exam questionaires, little tales, sheer cries of frustration, so that formally the book tries a number of modes, but the basic rage informing them all irons out the differences. And though the sarcasm is often intense, what I miss that so energizes her earlier volume is the liberating laughter. Perhaps, given the subject matter — patriarchal, church supported marriage as a hideous trap for women — the poet simply can't find anything funny in it. Yet some of the most powerfully angry writing I have read has also had its lightning flashes of (admittedly black) comedy; and this was certainly the case in Melfi's last book. Partly because the whole volume is on a single subject and partly because it's pitched in a single key, it fails to sustain my emotional commitment as I read. One can hope, however, that having gotten it out of her system, Melfi will return to the more complex vision she showed she was capable of in her last book.

George Melnyk is best known as the founding editor of *NeWest Review* and as a committed commentator on the concept of "radical regionalism." It comes as no surprise, then, to find his central obsessions at the heart of the plain and often moving poems of *The Empty Quarter* (Sidereal Press, 1983). The title poem, with its formal repetition and incremental accusations can stand for the whole: "a coin / without a face / is a slug" it begins, in order to transform its title back to money from the economics of farming. Elsewhere he writes of natives and Third World people, of the Irish problem, and in a shift of focus, of the momentary physical joy of swinging his son through the air while "wind swept your eyes / with clouds as you circled / the earth in my arms flying." The ambiguities here reach for a more complex poetic than do most of Melnyk's pieces, but everywhere the wise love of the man for his fellow man shines through.

A.F. Moritz has published a number of small pamphlets, but *The Visitation* (Aya Press, 1983) is his first major collection. One of its poems is titled "Keats in Rome," and the allusions of the title alone offer a neat and fitting analysis of this contemporary poet's subjects and approach to his materials. For Moritz shares much with the Romantics, including a vividly metaphoric imagination and a fascination with what remains from the past. But he is also a modern poet, an inheritor especially of the lessons Pound taught in his *Personae*. Indeed, this book is a quick-change artist's tour of a myriad of masks, calling to us from those frozen moments of arresting, and arrested, gesture which demand an attentive ear.

Moritz's people want to be heard; they have their illuminations, great or small, and they want to reflect the light. Yet they often stand in ironic relation to the meanings they speak and may not fully comprehend. "Capriccio of Roman Ruins" seems a paradigmatic Moritz poem:

> We, the living ones, are distinguishable
> from those we move among, people of stone,
> by the red and blue of our robes,
> the blood-glow of face and arm.
> We lounge on the worn steps beneath
> the last arch of a shattered roof
> where the vegetation hangs, and two of us
> are arguing a point, gesturing
> to the empty pure blue sky. Another, alone,
> dangles his feet in a little pool of rain water,
> leaning against a toppled frieze; and one walks,
> very slowly, back and forth, before the breached
> dome of a tomb. But in the frieze
> those others, grey or white, in colorless
> garments of rock, are lounging
> on their elbows by a little pool.
> Or on the surface of a huge urn, filled now
> with accidental dust and vines,
> those carved ones talk and circle slowly
> through eroded facades and marble alleys.
> And one of them, a naked giant,
> leans idly as though to mock us
> against a broken column already a ruin
> long centuries ago, when first he relaxed
> and upright, with open eyes, here fell asleep.

Many other speakers of varying interest inhabit this volume. There are also two longer poems. "You, Whoever You Are" intrigues because it insists on the radical anonymity of its speaker and those he addresses, but it never quite comes into focus. Moritz works better with characters, given figure from myth, legend, or story. The title poem is a long and unnerving monologue, supposedly what Elizabeth "spoke out with a loud voice" when Mary visited her. At its best, it touches the nerves, invoking a mystery more terrifying than the New Testament, at any rate, usually acknowledges. In poems like this, Moritz finds the still pulsating life of a traditional poetic discourse and brings it fully awake.

Roberta Morris's *Married Sisters* (Barton Press, 1981) is a slim collection of poems, verses, and prose pieces. It is also slyly illustrated by Pat Jeffries. Although Kay Armitage compares her work to Margaret Atwood's, I would argue that at its best it has a gentle yet tough humour that is quite different from Atwood's.

Probably the best piece of sustained writing in the book is the five part title piece: the prose is apparently transparent, but the witty and sometimes savage insights feel earned. A number of rhyming verses are cute but lack real fire. That can be felt in "Faking," "It didn't happen," and "Talk." Throughout, Morris assumes a casual tone of voice that disarms the reader, but she often offers stinging perceptions. Despite some typographical errors and a few too easy verses, *Married Sisters* attests to a real talent, one from which we will surely hear again.

The title poem of Stephen Morrissey's *Divisions* (Coach House, 1983) immediately announces the deeply personal — what Louis Dudek goes so far as to say is the "confessional" — nature of this collection. If Morrissey's earlier *The Trees of Unknowing* found a variety of means to distance the "I" even as it also insisted on an acute vision, these new poems foreground the poet's seemingly untranslated ego struggling with the forces of memory and pain.

"Divisions," for example, runs ragged through a past of denials. A powerful if sometimes awkward poem, it chooses awkwardness to signal the integrity of the personality roughly translating the inchoate knowledge memory brings to light. The poet will insist on the necessity of poetry — "only poetry justifies language / and when poetry ceases / there is disharmony" — yet he begins by admitting that even he had used writing as a way to deny relationships: "the last 12 years / I've kept a diary / everyday all 6,316 / pages of scribbling // & learnt nothing." But the poem enters the remembered denials of connection in order to deny them continuing power now. The deaths of his father and stepfather, the losses in friendship and love, these are recalled so carefully in order that he might go beyond them. "I would lie upon the earth // as upon your body // to embrace what I have not had // stars   raiment   darkness // *21 years of separation* // the pain the pain the pain."

In the poems which follow, Morrissey calls upon language and poetry to explore "those // unexplored areas of // civilization that have // long been turned under // the soil." Some of those "unexplored areas" are inhabited by "the dead in my life," and the book gathers force as a kind of exorcism that he and his age demand because he's a father now and does not wish to visit on the next generation the negations that so affected his youth. "Running," another long poem, moves with extreme slow pacing to confront his father's death and to insist that he "will // live // twice // your age // running // along."

66

In many ways the poems of *Division* are simpler and more accessible than the poems of *The Trees of Unknowing,* yet the sense of mystery in the world is the same in both books. The earlier poems sought to articulate that mystery with purity; the poems of *Divisions* seek to address it personally. They do so, on the whole, in a convincing and moving manner. The poet's willingness to appear naked in these poems, in an age when duplicitous personae abound, is courageous; but without a fine lyric gift to carry the honesty, there wouldn't be much to praise. There is.

Colin Morton's *Poem Without Shame* (Ouroboros, 1983) is another small pamphlet from the small Ottawa publisher which began last year. It's fun, and certainly worth the half-dollar. In essence a long and querulously surreal list, it would make a great piece for performance, yet there is a serious undercurrent to its apparent ramblings. Morton has also created some neat poetry postcards and bookmarks — concrete poems to put to use. I like the wry intelligence that informs both the various pieces and the impractical-practical uses he seeks to put them to.

The title poem of *Settlement in a School of Whales* (Fiddlehead Poetry Books, 1983) offers a good overview of Roger Nash's method: the poem rushes forward, almost tripping over its continually shifting metaphors, full of brio and comic extravagance — Sudbury *is* a settlement in a school of whales, the land is metamorphosed into ocean, nothing is fixed in this imaginative vision. For Nash everything lives, and actively, too. As "The rocks eat breakfast" shows, 'inanimate' is a term he refuses to understand: "The rocks gnaw light down out / of the sky and suck on it, slurp sparkles off / the lake, and graze on the glitter of house windows."

Born in England, Nash now teaches philosophy at Laurentian University and travels to the prairies and the big city of Toronto. Everywhere he goes, he applies his comic eye and his ear for rich colloquialisms mixed with eccentric but accurate metaphors. His "Two prairie sky poems" capture the feel of that qualitatively different atmosphere better than many prairie poets have managed to do. His "Two poems about nothing" delightfully engage the comic potential of their philosophical paradox.

Not everything in this book works equally well, and Nash is occasionally guilty of a certain sloppiness and looseness. But even these faults seem to fit the generally genial expansiveness of his poetry. And always the energy of invention, the sheer delight in demonstrating in the language the multiplicity of life, carries the reader on. Besides, I can forgive a poet a great deal who can write (albeit only one) "Sermon of a cricket in an empty bucket", and with Nash I don't have to:

> Krikakrik okrakofu!
> Okrassalo ossolim ssokra?
> Oloim akrosazi cimbalom jedda:
> zambezi zucchini ikriki.

Zither ikriki, zither jibuti:
jhelum zigzago, zero zenana.
Zulu zaggreb aka Crakow pikasso?
Krika pikolo, krikapikasso,
zebra paprika kirkakokafu!
Jigajig zion, jug-jug-jug.

This is a highly entertaining introduction to the work of a poet I suspect we'll be hearing from again. Such vitality will not, I think, remain silent for long.

Sharon H. Nelson announces her angrily ironic stance in the title of her latest book, *Mad Women & Crazy Ladies* (Sunken Forum Press, 1983), and she delivers on the tough promise of that title in most of the poems which follow. What helps to make the poems work is her tone—savage, ironic, witty, comic, exasperated, and even loving, by turns. She seeks to undercut the myths by which women have been understood. As she says in the title poem, "The women are mad, / quite mad. This explains everything." But no longer; no, the explanations will no longer suffice, so Nelson seeks to see beneath the surface of such explanations and to speak what she finds there.

Irony may, as someone once said, be the trope of slavery, but I don't think that's wholly so. Nelson at any rate can make of it a liberating gesture, as in "A Footstool in Heaven," which takes its title from a Talmudic saying to the effect that "the reward of a good wife is that she will be her husband's footstool in heaven." In this and other poems, Nelson records the pain and anger of women whom circumstances have forced to be footstools but who do not enjoy the feeling.

Two longer poems are especially powerful in their minimal and taut expressiveness. "Rite of passage" concerns the Jewish rite of growing long hair and then cutting it for marriage. "'All the Dead Dears,' a biography" is a poignant imagistic narrative on the suicide of Slyvia Plath. In these and in such other poems as "Farm Report," Nelson adopts various guises; she appears to see her duty as speaking for and in the putative voices of those who cannot articulate their own losses. It is a testament to the integrity of her vision and her craft that she carries out her task so well.

bp Nichol's *Continental Trance* (Oolichan Books, 1982) is the third book of *The Martyrology*, the ongoing monumental life work of one of our most important and inventive poets. The deliberately chosen context of the poem is a train journey from Vancouver to Toronto in July/August 1981, a reprise of a journey Nichol has made many times before. Yet the poem is utterly open to the contingent, and on a train the contingent is always present. Nichol even tells us of his revisions and what they signal. The saints reappear, as do the continuing necessities of his own life with his pregnant wife, his friends and family, his history. As he realizes, even the poem he is writing is only a sign of "the literal metaphor or symbol // linear narrative of random sequential thots // accidents of geography, history & circumstance // the given".

Nichol continues to engage and question the given, and all the major concerns of *The Martyrology* continue to announce themselves here in various guises. The saints, the quality of a life lived in quest (ioning), our relation to a creator/power, the strength and goodness of human communion/ community, and the problems of mortality: Nichol once again investigates them all in *Continental Trance*. There is precise natural description, sharp observation of peoples' behaviour, some witty self-referential humour, and much more. Nichol investigates the question of geography and how it affects the writer, suggesting we should forget "biography when geography's the clue / locale & history of the clear 'you'." He admits the inevitable "failure" of the poem:

> is this the poem i wanted to write?
>
> it never is
>
> it's a thing of words
> construct of a conscious mind
>
> governed by the inevitable end-rime
> time

But he is not fazed by this any more. The poem will continue, as will his life. It has become such a huge structure that it is impersonal, despite the increasing pressure of the personal in it. As a glimpse of where the next large section of *The Martyrology* is going, *Continental Trance* is interesting; as a map of a soul in process it is a thoroughgoing delight. I remain convinced that Nichol's ongoing great poem is one of the major works of the imagination in contemporary literature.

In her first collection of poetry, *Ambergris Moon* (Thistledown Press, 1983), Brenda Niskala draws on her personal background in the area known as Big Valley, Saskatchewan. Especially in the first half of the book, she adopts a variety of voices to present aspects of the farming life with humour and compassion. "The hired man says," for instance, perfectly catches its speaker's tone of wonder as he gives examples of why "Arno's missus / she's fierce you know." This is prairie anecdotal poetry at its best. A comic rhyming poem is fun, but Niskala also strives to show the kinds of conflicts, especially between the young who wish to leave and the old who choose to stay.

The second half of *Ambergris Moon* is more concerned with the gray areas between thought and dream, circumstance and happenstance. One poem is called "Contemplation cycle," and its sudden shift from a world elsewhere to the pressing mortal here and now maps the process of many of these poems. The first poem stays firmly in the fantasy world; others never get there. Here, more often than in the first section, Niscala appears to write autobiographically, yet she is never simply confessional. Some of the poems seem to overstate the quality of the conflict they describe, but on the whole the strangeness-in-the-ordinary they seek to evoke comes through.

Niscala seems to have most control over her materials when she deals with remembered material, as in the best anecdotal poems here; she seems less sure with some of the more visionary pieces, and her tropes tend to be less precise and focused in them. Still, on the whole, *Ambergris Moon* is an interesting first step in a career that's bound to continue.

As his latest collection, *Whirlwinds* (Guernica Editions, 1983), demonstrates, Ken Norris remains a lyric poet in the grand tradition of the Troubadours, singing songs of love found, love lost, love ever-returning in one guise or another to the dedicated lover. Yet his poems are very much of the here and now: if he is a wandering lover with many loves, so are his ladies; if the world of economics, politics, and war impinges on all our lives, even those of lovers, then he will not only admit this but even push the point home (if only perhaps to make clear the inadequacy of art to deal with it) in such poems as "Poetic License." Essentially, however, *Whirlwinds*, like last year's *To Sleep, To Love*, is a book exploring the vagaries of modern love and the possibility that the feelings he celebrates are something less (or at least less committed).

The latter difficulty is taken up at length in the final poem, "Watching Leaves Fall," where Norris investigates the many meanings of the term through a series of epic lists where "pizza and ice cream," "Mickey Mantle above all other players," various sex acts with various partners, music, books, events, and much else are all equalized by the running title "I loved," the past tense itself adding to the unsureness the poem invokes, as much as the fact that the "you" he speaks to keeps shifting from one person to another. I find this a troublesome poem but that is probably because it is so honest, especially coming after a number of more conventional, if often lyrically acute, love poems, which it puts in question just as it puts the concept of love itself in question.

The poems in *Whirlwinds* vary widely in their style and power. There are a number of quite flat pieces as well as some delicate and moving ones. Norris is highly prolific and the inevitable sifting process will have to come later. The good poems are powerfully affective new versions of an ancient mode, including some interestingly self-conscious ones about the act of making poems out of making love. What finally raises this book above many others like it, however, is the way many of its poems, especially "Watching Leaves Fall," question the (possibly sexist) basis of such poems and such "love," not only in the case of this poet but throughout the history of this kind of poetry.

A large huzzah to Fiddlehead and editor Peter Thomas for publishing Alden Nowlan's *Early Poems* (Fiddlehead Poetry Books, 1983). Containing all the work the late Maritime poet had published by the age of thirty (in *The Rose and the Puritan* (1958), *A Darkness in the Earth* (1958), *Wind in a Rocky Country* (1960), *Under the Ice* (1961), *The Things Which Are* (1962), and *Five New Brunswick Poets* (1962)), it is a remarkable testament to the youthful flowering of a rich and brilliant talent. Since these books have long been out of print, *Early Poems* is a necessary book for any serious lover of Canadian poetry.

From the beginning of his publishing career, Nowlan displayed a tough, variously comic and tragic, but never sentimental understanding of and compassion for his subjects — the people of the small towns and farms where he had grown up and worked as a reporter. Indeed, his newspaper background probably accounts for the clarity and precision of his descriptions, but it's his poet's vision that finds articulation in the telling phrases that dig below the surface of things to reveal the profound human pain that seems to enter so many lives.

As the title of his earliest collection reveals, Nowlan always knew where that pain was rooted, for as one of the people he wrote about, he understood the emotional conflict between Puritan repression and instinctive fleshly desire. He also knew the fear of passion which drove the Puritan machine even if, as a poet, he knew the perilous beauty and freedom which waited just beyond the jail walls we erect around ourselves. In the title poem, the Puritan fears "the panthers" as well as "the girls in silken sins and jostled hair / who tempt me," but, as the rose says, "God is there, not here." It is a paradigmatic poem.

If Nowlan's Romantic vision goes back to Blake and beyond, his early understanding of his craft owes much to Frost and Masters. From Frost, especially, he learned to hone the ordinary speech of the Maritime people into the finely turned traditional stanzas, a verse form Nowlan would later eschew almost entirely for a rich and tale-ridden open verse. But later he would also write much more out of his personal life; what is so impressive about these early poems is how self-effacing he can be much of the time, giving voice to a remarkable gallery of characters, from Baptist ministers to the "Hungerfords, McGards and Staceys" at the "Stoney Ridge Dance Hall," and including such famous ones as "Warren Prior." Many of the others figured in the poems of *Under the Ice* deserve equal recognition with Warren, and that's another reason it is so good to have this book. For almost all the characters, the closed form of their verses perfectly mirrors the entrapment they feel. As Nowlan's speakers begin to seek greater freedom (often only to find themselves in subtler traps) in *The Things Which Are*, we see him experimenting with the more open line that was to become his trademark from the mid-sixties until his death.

There are some weak poems here, of course, and some examples of forced poetic diction — these are after all the poems of a writer still serving his apprenticeship to his craft — but such flaws are few indeed in comparison to the successes. *Early Poems* is a substantial and impressive collection, full of wit, irony, anger, love, and much else. Official religion comes off poorly, though Nowlan is usually satisfied to laugh and pity simultaneously, yet a genuine spirituality informs these poems. There were poems here I've remembered for twenty years since I first encountered them (not alas, in any of the original collections, or, if so, only on loan), like "Looking for Nancy," and some of the others I've mentioned, but there were many others I had not read before which also profoundly touched me. All of these poems express a double vision which "The Rose and the Puritan" announced so clearly at the beginning of his career. A lovely later poem, "Picking Raspberries," from 1962, offers another version of that double vision, one of only many in this major gathering of the early poems of a man whose tragic death at the age of fifty robbed us of who knows how much more. In the face of that loss, poems such as this remind us of how much he accomplished:

> Noon.
> But it is twilight
> here
> inside the
> raspberry thicket.
> Green-black leaves
> dull the nail-tipped
> arrows of the sun
> so they caress.
>
> We won't feel the thorns
> for hours yet;
> tonight
> I will bathe
> the hot scars
> on her back and legs
> with cool liquids. Now
>
> the sweet berries
> break
> apart
> on our tongues.

The photographs by R.E. Balch enhance but do not distract from the text. There are, alas, some typos, a few of which definitely interfere with the meaning of the poems. Nevertheless, Nowlan's *Early Poems* are not to be missed.

Don Polson is something of a Wordsworthian Romantic, caught in the Windsor Western Hospital Centre where he sees the human condition at its worst and most resilient, then escaping to the countryside where nature offers him much the same solace it offered another escapee from the city nearly two centuries ago. In *Moving Through Deep Snow* (Thistledown Press, 1984), Polson offers poems from both realms of his experiences, heaven and hell balancing each other out.

Indeed, as many of his reminiscent poems make clear, the imagery of the Bible is familiar ground for Polson, but it does its best work when only implied, as in most of the poems in the third section, "The Clear Eye of Our Neighbour." These poems are mostly based on people he has dealt with as a social worker, and Polson often manages to catch their tone and bitter wit tellingly. These are surely the poems that lead the Thistledown editors to compare Polson to the late Alden Nowlan. The comparison is apt, but Polson lacks the cutting edge of Nowlan's compassion, as a comparison of the quite similar poems, Polson's "The Stigmata" and Nowlan's "Daughter of Zion" demonstrates. On the other hand, Polson's remarkably sympathetic catching of a young women's story in "On that Night of Freezing Rain" makes for a powerfully understated poem.

Elsewhere Polson writes of family feelings as both father and son, and of the pleasures of the great outdoors. I find that his sense of the line is often awkward but the integrity of his feelings is generally clearly expressed. Nevertheless, many of these poems fail to come alive for me; as short personal essays, they have their charm, but they don't dance. Every so often, one does dance, and the resulting charge is very satisfying. "Old Barn, Durham County" is a marvelous small poem of images energized; in poems like this Polson achieves something of which even Wordsworth might be proud.

On the basis of his first major collection, *Kiss Me Down to Size* (Thistledown Press, 1983) I would call Ken Rivard a foothills surrealist of sorts. The poems in this book speak in a variety of voices, from a wide range of occupations and preoccupations, but they often go on too long for their own good.

Beginning with some warm if occasionally obscure poems about his daughter's dreams and nightmares, Rivard suddenly shifts gears with an unsettling comic poem addressed to a rapist. Following this, Rivard addresses a series of poems to particular people and then moves to more specific accounts of his perceptions of the surrounding world. A lengthy narrative sequence about being a CPR cop achieves both comedy and anecdotal clarity. The poems which follow contain other tales of work and the various individuals he meets there. They are enjoyable as tales but don't always work as poems.

Rivard's genial sense of the people he runs into informs the whole book. He likes them for their individual foibles and he offers us glimpses of those foibles in the poems. Sometimes his comparisons seem strained, and I find he holds my attention most when he pays strict attention to his subject without reaching for far out analogies. All in all, *Kiss Me Down to Size* is an entertaining debut which could have benefited from tighter editing.

In *Brides of the Stream* (Oolichan Books, 1983), his first book in three years, Joe Rosenblatt returns to his earliest concerns as a poet, though with something of a change in focus. Rosenblatt has been living on Vancouver Island for some time now, and has taken up fly fishing for trout, an activity which provides the context for this sequence of prose and poetry. Paying (sometimes parodic) homage to such earlier philosophers of the sport as Isaac Walton and Roderick Haig-Brown, *Brides of the Stream* also continues Rosenblatt's wierdly erotic investigation of animal living from the imagined inside.

Since *The LSD Leacock* in 1963 and its explorations of such mysteries as "How Mice Make Love," Rosenblatt has not shied away from bravely seeking out the roots (and branches) of the erotic lives of animals, birds, insects, and fish; but what's new in *Brides of the Stream* is the erotic/violent link between him as fisherman and them as both seductive beauties and potential food. The poems adopt various strategies and points of view. "Uncle Nathan," a smart and tough old trout, won't be fooled when younger ones take the lure. All the fish dream of and eat the flies, worms, and grasshoppers which come too near. Sex *is* death in the dream-like world of the stream. Sometimes, anyway.

Many of the poems are dreams, of either the fish or the man. Images from the opposing worlds mingle and mate, producing strange offspring in the unconscious. If fishing is like sex, it's also like writing. Rosenblatt teases at these obscure connections and teases us with hints of some fuller insight into their meaning. I'm not sure he ever achieves it.

The best pieces in the book are lovingly detailed descriptions of the stream he fished and the life he so carefully observed there. Though the style is pure Rosenblatt, the way of attention, the meditative precision of focus is shared with the great nature writers allusively acknowledged at various points. Possibly because it marks something of a new direction in his work, and possibly because it is an attempt at a long poem which doesn't quite cohere as such, *Brides of the Stream* isn't Rosenblatt's most successful work, but it's a fascinating one, and in its best passages it's violently beautiful, wierdly disturbing.

God Loves Us Like Earthworms Love Wood (Porcupine's Quill, 1983) is good advertising for the collection of poems it names, for it signals clearly their general subject matter and technique. This latest book by Allan Safarik is a kind of modern bestiary, and Safarik generally explains or ironically points up the various analogies he offers us throughout. In "Crimes Against the State," for example, he suggests that "politics and biology / concur briefly" in a particular situation, imaged, as always in these poems, in either a realistic or surrealistic image from the animal world.

Many of these poems display a sharply defined imagery of the kind one recalls from *Okira*, Safarik's first, Japanese-influenced book. Simultaneously, however, they will also sport dubious and often flat similes which seek to be strangely compelling but are only oddly askew: "And the horse's cock / extends below his belly / like a handshake / draining the fields." Safarik's poems attempt to achieve a bitterly realist vision of the power politics that enters all human relations. Some of his tales of animal behaviour, like "The Dead Man's Eye" and "The Natural Case History of the North American Rat," achieve the intensity he seeks, but for the most part these poems fail to ignite, despite their fiery intentions.

While admitting that the poems of St. John Simmons are often powerfully evocative in their manipulation of nature imagery, I also must say they tend to arouse a kind of disgust in me. It is interesting that the first and last poems in his first collection, *Wilderness Images* (Fiddlehead Poetry Books, 1983), "Domaine Perdu" and "The Children Asked Me to Kill You," are concerned with the death and mutilation of women. This image of woman as powerful and therefore dangerous, frightening, and to be feared and attacked, hovers like a ghost over a majority of these poems. In "The Invention of the Mystical Beasts," the narrative consciousness of the poem "understands the earth / is a woman," but having done so seeks to "satisfie her / with the temples made from her bones" (and one is forced to ask, "satisfie whom?". "In Domaine Perdu," a woman's body is cast in pieces across the landscape, as if only in such dispersal could she be loved.

These poems are full of violence, often rendered with exquisite precision. I'm not sure what message Simmons thinks he's signalling with his tales of sexual carnage in nature, but the one I receive is frighteningly misogynist as it builds to that final poem. There, having left the women to "die of beauty" in the woods, the speaker returns, saying "I will lift you up and love you / . . . / but you will not see, you will not." Then he takes "some few bones back / bones so white and smooth / . . . / and I will hang them in the yard / where the children, happy in their stoic innocence, / may ring them like Buddhist chimes." The tone here reaches for a cool objectivity; the narrative, emerging from the fearful and hateful confrontations throughout the book, signs another kind of "love," one I simply cannot accept.

In *Wordsong: Twelve Ballads* (Sono Nis Press, 1983), Robin Skelton has gathered and ordered a group of poems he admits do not fit in with the poems he is collecting for the volume of Longer Poems to stand beside his *Collected Shorter Poems*. Most of these poems were published in an out-of-print English collection in 1960; the others appeared before the end of that decade. As he admits, they are "more rhetorical" than his recent work, "frequently rambustious, and sometimes bawdy." They are also fine examples of the modern ballad form.

Skelton has always been a good craftsman, especially when working in traditional forms. For the reader who feels uncomfortable with poems based on the traditional ballad, in which a speaker, often mysterious or in touch with the supernatural, tells of strange happenings in a mine, at sea, or just in dreams, these poems will have little to offer. But Skelton knows what he's about, and whether he's engaging the muse as goddess-whore, telling the sad story of Billy Barker who found gold but died penniless in a Victoria Old Men's Home, or speaking for such abstract figures as Need or Fulfillment, he keeps these verses moving, with lots of well-wrought tropes and teasing implications. Throughout, the importance of the telling is insisted upon, especially in the two ballads to the Muse; these speakers are all poets of a kind; they all want to be heard, and Skelton captures that urgency in his verses.

Word Song is not for everyone, but it is a good example of what a writer trained in traditional craft can do with one of the many formal structures he has inherited. These are ballads, articulating the traditional concerns of ballads, yet they are also poems of the twentieth century, and no one would mistake them for aught else. Their real interest lies in that intriguing mixture of past and present which they speak.

As well as writing poetry, Robin Skelton has been creating collages since the late 1940s. *House of Dreams* (Porcupine's Quill, 1983) collects 48 of his favorite pieces, accompanied by short commentaries which he insists are those "of a partially informed docent wandering around an exhibition by someone else."

Like his best poems, these collages contain witty, sometimes disturbing, juxtapositions of imagery; there are visual puns and rhymes within the pictures, and many of the specific images have mythic or religious symbolic overtones. Skelton's commentaries usually alert us to major possible significances, as when he tells us that three naked women represent the triple goddess (a figure who appears throughout his poetry).

In Percy Jarrett's stunning photographs, Skelton's collages are certainly impressive in their stark contrasts and occasionally startling, receding depths. Despite the many naked women (most of whom appear to have been snipped out of *Playboy*), they maintain a strict austerity, and as a reflection of another aspect of this well-known poet's creativity, they offer both further insights into his psyche and some iconography of undeniable power.

Although *In the Eye of the Bee* (rdc press, 1983) is her fourth book of poetry, it is perhaps the first book by Marion Smith to have a chance at national distribution, since her publisher, rdc press, seems to be trying to reach a wider reading public. In it, Smith speaks as an elder of the tribe, a woman approaching death but not yet quite ready to embrace it. Although she scatters a sequence of poems, "A Day's Lifetime," throughout the book, Smith is essentially a traditional lyric poet, looking at the natural world and reading allegories in its various occurrences.

Hers is a poetry of plain and ordinary speech, and though this is a strength in that it reflects the integrity of the wisdom she has gained through long living, it is something of a weakness insofar as her verses seldom sing or dance. What she says is interesting, but not as poetry so much as thoughtful observation. This criticism applies especially to "A Day's Lifetime," which literally articulates her thoughts during one day as she recalls her life on the farm with her late husband and her children, ponders the meaning of the life she has lived and continues to live, and wonders at the inability of the young — in this case a granddaughter — to perceive that the old are not a different species but what they will one day become. These ruminations, and some of the dark instances of dream and insight in the other poems, move me with their honesty, yet I find that they lack that extra transformative and rhythmic power which pushes verse into poetry.

Although it's often true that the wisdom we wish for does not come with age, it is indeed a pleasure to meet with it when it does, as, for example, in Frances Sparshott's most recent book *The Cave of Trophonius and other poems* (Brick Books, 1983). Partly I recognize wisdom because I hear it in the unsentimental laughter which echoes in the background of these poems, which are fully self-aware yet never less than wholly attentive to the world as it paces us towards the inevitable grave.

There are four sequences in this collection and each one offers its own prickly perk of pleasure (and perhaps pain). "Stations of Loss" begins with "Growing older is this — / nothing really, / folks do it every day / who can't do anything else at all hardly": a personal statement surely, yet the person is shifty, and the poem quickly transcends autobiographical self-pity. It gets funnier and bleaker with each passing fragment yet it is also compassionate in an austere way. "At a Later Symposium" offers some further tales of Socrates' encounter with the priestess Diotima. Both she and he appear to tread landscapes and cityscapes less localized in time than we would expect. A note of mystery is sounded here which the next two poems will explore further. "Netsuke" is a suite of haiku-like poems, some of which use images in the traditional manner to evoke ideation, others of which entertain the ideas directly. Again a profound, sometimes gnomic, sense of play informs the poems, as in "Bricklayers not architects / pleased my tutor who is dead," where the syntax's deliberate ambiguity adds to the mysteries of the whole.

That mysterioso is given full rein in the title poem, a meditation of sorts on the tale of the oracle. Again, Sparshott weaves images of ancient and modern life into one oddly satisfying whole. The personal and legendary meet, some dark knowledge which resists interpretation is imparted, the poem *reveals* aspects of the darkness we all must face. As I said, a wise book, albeit an often comically entertaining one. Possibly the best writing Sparshott has yet done.

In *Bourgeois Pleasures* (Quarry Press, 1984), Ken Stange writes a long letter to a person he has created. A mix of prose and verse, this letter discusses creator's and created's lifestyles and philosophies and explores the reasons for creating (some of the reasons). As Stange says in an Author's Note, he believes "that literature, like science, is a way of exploring different perspectives," and that the results of any single exploration are always tentative. He calls all his books hypotheses and this is Hypothesis 7. And as he is keen to point out, it contradicts earlier ones, which sought to explore the Primitive in terms of Canada's North.

Bourgeois Pleasures is something of an attempt to write a witty *apologia pro vita sua*. Stange invents both himself (the "Ken Stange" who writes the letter) and his audience (the Benjamin who receives it as well as his three lovers). Having set up a nice paradoxical situation, Stange then seeks to explore and exploit it through further paradoxical discussion. His wit is sometimes heavy-handed but it is dealing with a weighty subject. What are Bourgeois Pleasures, anyway, and why should a poet accept, and even revel in, his bourgeois lifestyle? Stange makes a good argument for the bourgeoisie as the only class with real "potential for empathy, for real intelligence, for art. That most fail to realize this potential is no criticism." And it is his varied versions of the poet's apprehension of the physical world, of passion, and of philosophical speculation which lends his book its charm.

The poems are set in place, in the ongoing argument, as *exemplae*, and they serve that purpose well. Nevertheless, I can't help feeling at times that the whole, including, or especially, the poems, is planned too carefully. Stange has a good sense of image and I enjoy most those poems which invest images with their own numinosity without trying to turn them to an ulterior purpose. But the larger purpose of testing the hypothesis constrains him throughout. Within the self-imposed limits of his fiction, Stange has created an intriguing essay on the forces which govern the act of poetry. With all its flaws, *Bourgeois Pleasures* offers its own intellectual pleasures to its readers.

For George Stanley, the poetical and the political are inseparable. In all their variety of tone and form, the poems of *Opening Day* (Oolichan Books, 1983) insist that art is grounded in the lives we lead, and those lives have political and economic contexts, whether we recognize them or not. This attitude could make for some overly didactic proselytizing verse, and occasionally does, but usually Stanley's sense of humour or his apprehension of transcendental possibilities raises his poems beyond mere essays on a theme.

The sense of humour, often grimly ironic, leads Stanley to write the many near-ballads which inhabit this book. Sometimes they're pure slapstick; sometimes, as in "Down in the Fla," they dig beneath the surface of the work-a-day world to uncover what lies hidden in the dreams the workers enact. Stanley is also a master of the throwaway ending, the very

arbitrary absurdity of which calls the whole poem into question — as he
intends it to. The apparently inconsequential poems in which he does this
are an attempt to create occasional poems out of the most private occasions
— to leave them at that level of importance yet somehow claim importance
for them. Usually, he succeeds.

These, one might call them "lighter," poems provide a kind of frame
for the major works of *Opening Day*: the title poem, "Youth," and "Paradise
Shelter," a moving elegy for Russell Fitzgerald, the sculptor. There's also
a group of specifically analytical political poems at the end of the book
which keep slipping into mere essays but are occasionally powerful in their
bitter insights into how capitalist materialism robs the world of its value.
"Youth" and "Paradise Shelter" engage the political realities the other poems
argue about, but they go further, reaching for a spiritual mystery, the
presence of which generates tremendous power in the poems. In the elegy
the poet says, "Whatever this place is / that we will not admit / to each
other we have discovered / is all there is." But "all there is" opens outward
in these poems, which is why they are so rich in implication.

Although both the kinds and the quality of the poems in *Opening Day*
vary widely, the book exerts a real charm. Stanley's vision has integrity
as he continues to seek the human possibilities in a world almost lost in
the babble of advertising gimmickry. As poet, he fights to keep the language
human.

In his review of Andrew Suknaski's *Montage for an Interstellar Cry* (Turnstone Press, 1982), Robert Kroetsch praises the poem's "energy", "wildness,"
and "urge to kick out the jams." All of which are fully present, uninhibited,
despite Kroetsch's reservations on the subject, through the extensive editing
by David Arnason and David Carr.

Rooted in the place and time of Winnipeg during Suknaski's tenure as
Writer-in-Residence at the University of Manitoba, the poem casts back
through memory, history and myth, as well as spreading out in space to
other parts of Canada, Dresden, Hiroshima, and Pinochet's Chile. It features
many speakers besides the author (who appears as "suknatskyj," while
they are given equally outrageous names based on Indian mythology or
Ukrainian spelling).

The poem is truly a montage, especially in the fourth sense my dictionary
gives: "any combination of disparate elements that forms or is felt to form
a unified whole, single image, etc." Yet a reader feels compelled to ask,
"is *felt* to form a unified whole" by whom? Suknaski appears to want to
stuff everything into this poem, and while the effort to do so manifests
immense imaginative energy, I'm not sure it works completely. Ancient
Norse mythlogy, histories of war's terror, tales of torture, the story of a
fellow poet's search for his birth-mother (which that poet has told in his
own book), anecdotes of drinking and wenching, philosophizing, moralizing
and much else jostle and strive to hold our attention. The poem flexes
its muscles all over the page, ranging from anger to joy, pain to pleasure

in tone. The "cry" of the title, though it makes many significant appearances throughout, is finally summed up in an angry monologue by the poet's friend:

> . . . all i wanna say is
> we've all got the right
> the right of the cry
> that pregnant women
> the void an i humiliated
> needlessly
> she has
> the right of the cry
> . . . an my woman
> trying to push one of the three women
> into the new snow by the river
> my woman has
> the right of the cry
> . . . you have
> the right of the cry
> we all have
> the right of the cry
>
> that's all we've got man
> in this abyss

In a sense he's right; as the poem has shown it, all we face *is* an abyss. Or perhaps not. The energy of the exploration, even of the horror, argues another possibility, a possibility discovered in the rest of the title — that which, gathered and collaged together, finally reaches the stars may articulate our full humanity. Perhaps the cry will be as much of welcome as for help.

So, Suknaski provokes me with his near-chaotic riches. Yet a part of me remains aloof, moved by the wild intensity of the poem, but often wishing for still greater artistic control and focus. Nevertheless, despite its flaws, the book has something to say. Its experiments deserve our attention.

George Swede has published many of his haiku-like poems in the various journals dedicated to that sort of thing. As I have said before, to make a book of haiku work is a difficult thing, at least for a contemporary poet writing in English; I at least am easily bored by too much of the same thing, and there simply aren't that many poems like "In a Station of the Metro." All of which stands as prologue to my saying that in *Flaking Paint* (Underwhich Editions, 1983), a tiny pamphlet of one-line bits, Swede has deconstructed the standard English haiku, in a very interesting fashion.

Oh, there are a few obvious pieces here, like "in the bathroom mirror the parallel universe," which appears on a right hand page; but it's the left hand pages which are most interesting, as in this opposite: "des ert crow ded wi thsp ace." In these poems, the words lose much of their standard referentiality, slipping the nets of signification. We sound them, we watch them dissolve, and something emerges like the original work beneath the "flaking paint" of the title. Swede doesn't overstay his welcome with these tidbits, and as a result *Flaking Paint* is an enjoyable and engaging little book.

Anne Szumigalski's *Risks* (rdc press, 1983) is a long comic poem which playfully questions the *acts* of the imagination upon which all art rests, and where they lead. If "as a flake rests / on the tip of a finger / explains L, so a phrase / rests on the tip of the mind," then, once tipped, the mind tumbles into a free flowing stream of conscious and unconscious images and punning changes of seen. L, the lover, poet, critic, transposes his life and dreams into stories of adventure, love, and the difficulties of creation. Szumigalski takes delight in following the turns of language from one situation to another, yet she maintains them all within L's consciousness.

Both L and Szumigalski are aware of the power of analogy, but L is still trapped in what he calls the "listed similes" of the old masters, which bring "to mind the familiar / snaking highways and byways of the / tradition-oriented thought-process." Szumigalski knows these routes, too, but she is more interested in getting off them onto less travelled back roads. Although "L is forced to recant / he swears off poetics forever," Szumigalski keeps him *in* them and pushes him further, through even more transformations of traditional metaphors, right back to where he began in the snow: "he pokes one finger gingerly out / into the falling snow / he has to wait several minutes / before a single crusty flake / floats down and settles / on his fingertip." Intriguingly, L is back in the real world, too. Accompanied by Jim Westergard's evocative illustrations, *Risks* is an entertaining, witty view of the artistic process.

"Discourse," the title of one of the poems in Sharon Thesen's second major collection, *Holding the Pose* (Coach House Press, 1983), clearly signals the self-awareness and self-analysis with which the poet approaches her task, and provides a clue as to how these often toughly lyrical poems call into question the very nature and validity of "lyric." "The small vocabulary / of love needs its own / thin blue dictionary," she says; and on one level many of the poems in this powerful, and complex, and engaging book seek to discover words for that dictionary.

The first section of *Holding the Pose*, "Sheet Music," is rooted in popular song, the often banal lyrics lying (in wait) to keep us all in thrall to something old and raw and intimate." "Twisted" gets at the core of the problem, and in its witty twists and turns on familiar conventions it also demonstrates Thesen's superb handling of idiom:

Suffering a temporary
failure of imagination
the composer composes
a love song.

In which Mr. Mahoo Baja
a recent immigrant
takes a hotel room
& phones up the sister
of a friend

After the scene
in the steambath
the friend's sister
departs in a hurry.

The composer wasted.
Up all night long
trying to rhyme
what happened.
Trying to make love
& anguish out of
real life.

Love, then, and how "the sentimental beast" continues to exploit us all, is one of the major themes of *Holding the Pose*; another is how private anguish and public (political) unconcern engage each other in our culture. Thesen doesn't pretend to hold answers no one has, but she does respond to the realities, and with a greater sensitivity to the personal nuances of language than many of her contemporaries. In "X," her poem for and from Jacobo Timerman, she faces up to the duplicities of writing and still finds an affirmation of its necessity; for even if the act is only "a beating thing at the typewriter," nevertheless, as she says to a fellow poet, "you are, we are, wedded to it." So love and language meet in desire's grip, its need to "imagine a better future" no matter that we "do / not transform a single fact."

Thesen has a wicked sense of the absurd and comic aspects of even the most emotionally painful moments. She is only too aware of the potential for failure in all human arrangements and relationships, yet even in "Long Distance: An Octave," which clearly limns the difficulties of communication, let alone the communion of love, she affirms:

We talk anyway
being human &
a fine morning
promising the blooming

of dandelions, ornamental
bushes called everlasting
beauty & so forth.

And earlier in that same fine sequence she insists — with a graceful nod
of acknowledgement to but not necessarily agreement with Rilke — that
it is in this world that whatever pleasure or grace we find lies:

The enchanted
body sings.

At the centre
of the garden

a sculpted angel
from many angles

seems to dance:
material, loving.

Some of that pleasure will always come, I believe, from art, from poetry.
And Sharon Thesen is one of the poets whose work never fails to exhilarate
me. In the delicate tensions of her discourse lie truths no other speech
but poetry can contain. *Holding the Pose* is confirmation of a major talent.

Colleen Thibaudeau is a precious poetic resource: I can think of no one
writing today who so domesticates the magical. In her first collection since
My granddaughters are combing out their long hair, Thibaudeau offers found
poems, sound poems, parodics, and the usual gamut of poems in which
strangers from various levels of being — from comic strips, books, and
films, from the recesses of memory, or from just down the street — "make
their first acquaintance here in a blur of words." Colleen Thibaudeau's *The
Martha Landscapes* (Brick Books, 1984) is not to be missed.

Thibaudeau could be called a regionalist, I suppose, since so many of
her poems are rooted in the Southwestern Ontario landscape near her home
in London. But her real region is the imagination, and she continually
explores it with a heartfelt compassion for its inhabitants which is always
present but never directly spoken of in the poems. That she also has a
marvelously awry sense of humour, often emerging in moments where
particular human pain is manifest, is but one more sign of her special mastery.

A number of the poems in *The Martha Landscapes* are wrought of
recollections of childhood and youth. Some, like "The Tin Shop" and
"Bentie's Palaces," simply invest the remembered past with an articulate
significance only the older poet writing could read there. Others, like the
hugely compassionate "Sociable People Wondering What I Do," gather then

and now, with their crazy oppositions and troubling insistences that inside there is no change, grow into a pattern of affirmation-despite-all.

Thibaudeau's titles help to prepare a reader for the shifting and startlingly clear but mysterious landscape of her poems — "The Beautiful Horses of the Camargue," "Inwhich I Become Confused, the End of the World Being Imminent," "Notes for the crash sequence in *Poet to Tower*" — but finally you have to read the poems to experience their particularized magic. "My Grandmother's Sugar Shell, Ontario Baroque" provides a good introduction to Thibaudeau's unique and delightfully humane poetry:

> My grandmother's sugar shell (spoon), Ontario Baroque, has just fallen
> out of the uncleaned silver bag.
> What does it mean, I wonder
> One day only I saw her stop work.
> We lay out on the grass by the highway under the big maple
> and two cars went by toward Owen Sound. When she heard
> their car coming for dinner, she got up, a big woman
> with Scottish shoulders, built too heavy on the top like
> all the Stewarts, her leg-bones stilt-like in proportion
> to the square rest of her
>   And she rose all of a piece,
> I remember that she rose up somehow straight and not
> hinging her knees, nor using her hands, nor her elbows,
> nor leaning her head forward. So that
> she was the reverse of a tree falling before a quick gust.
> That is, she rose on a slant as if pulleys were attached
> to her everywhere   or as if
> the kitchen woodstove were a magnet that suddenly
> drew her inside.   One minute she was
> all green and gold lying there dappled. The next
> she was half-way up the lawn and in motion over the steps.
> The door opened magically and she disappeared. She would
> never wonder about anything, just say "That spoon needs
> cleaning."
> And yet I think it means she needs remembering.

This is what *The Martha Landscapes* can do. It is how and why these poems remember that make this book so worthwhile.

Yvonne Trainer is a young poet from Southern Alberta who recently completed an M.A. in Creative Writing at UNB. It's not surprising her first book is from there. *Customers* (Fiddlehead Poetry Books, 1983) is an interesting attempt on her part to offer a coherent collection of poems, as it presents every occasion of a poem in terms of buying or selling. The first group of poems is from the point of view of a nervous child who mostly finds the marketplace alien and would rather be safe at home. Trainer captures the tone and mood of her childish persona with precision.

The longer group of poems which follows is not so cohesive. The concept of the title plays across them all, but the speakers range from sales people to customers to observers of the market scene. Some of the poems are finely etched vignettes, but some still feel unfinished to me, with their occasional loose similes and unfocused images. In her final poem, the poet argues that "It is a rule / All shoppers must carry / something" and then tells us that "Whatever I carry / must fit nicely / in the hollow / of my skull." What fits nicely includes a lot, and that promises well for the future of this young poet, even if I hope she'll pack more precise language and technique into her next foray.

Richard Truhlar's *Moon Dice* (Underwhich Editions, 1982) is a beautifully made pamphlet containing nine mysterious little poems, "homolinguistic translations," as the author says, of selections "from Albert Girand's 1884 volume *Pierrot Lunaire* which Arnold Schoenberg used for his famous song cycle of the same name." All of which is relevant information for it explains both the odd distance the poems maintain and their real but eccentric music (I'm assuming, of course, that Truhlar's base text is an English translation of Girard's original — hence "homolinguistic translations").

At any rate, these poems resist meaning yet offer glimpses of event. Such playful writing insists on the materiality of language. Words become opaque; the text represents nothing more than its shifting self. Strangely, although such writing is seldom *about* mysterious or fantastic realms, it evokes them by becoming itself mysterious in its resistance to traditional signification. Because Truhlar displays wit and aural subtlety in his com-position, *Moon Dice* is a satisfying subject (or object) of the reader's meditation.

In her third book, *The Little Flowers of Madame de Montespan* (Porcupine's Quill, 1983) Jane Urquhart has chosen to cast her alert gaze across the lives of Louis XIV and his court. It is *her* alert gaze but it is also that of the book's title figure. Creating an historical overlay of voices, Urquhart conjures up a deliberately indeterminate persona who can make free with history and historical consciousness: she is there and she sees how things are then; she is here and she sees what has become of the grandiose buildings, the massively elaborate constructs the king ordered into being.

Urquhart uses three forms of discourse here: gnomic verses, which offer moments of intense scrutiny and feeling; prose poems, whose numbered sections accumulate details of an arcane argument concerning ends and means, and the imaginative failures which follow from too much pressure on ends; and "Anonymous Journal" entries which appear to be reports from the present but contain overtones of Madame de Montespan inter-rogating her situation through a telescope provided by the erosion of time.

The king desires control: he seeks overwhelming order in place of unsanctioned growth, and all his buildings, including his nightmare construction of his own New France (doomed to nightly defeat), reflect his desire to impose geometry on the world of change. Urquhart brilliantly captures the scarred futility of the project in "Venetian Gondoliers at Versailles," which would be hilarious in its picture of wrongheadedness were it not so bitter in its presentation of imaginative loss. The desiccation of the king's emotional life is shown in "The King Advises his Son." "Never speak to women," Louis says, "never let them carry your secrets / they are lapses / barricade the entrance / . . . / give away nothing." This is the message of imaginative and emotional sterility, and it eventually infiltrates the whole court, even those who love him: Madame de Montespan wishing for him a poisoned shirt, telling us herself: "the mouth he puts to yours / contains a brutal statement / your limbs become machinery / to the limits he enforces."

Those limits are still signified in the geometric perfections of Versailles and Marly, but time insists on marring all with life: "The statues and the giant urns, they said, had somehow changed location in the last several years." Urquhart casts a cold eye on Louis XIV's attempt to preserve a monument to self against mutability, but she is not without compassion for his failure of nerve and imagination, even if her greater compassion is for her other voice, the woman who in her loving and child-bearing knows where the heart has gone wrong, gone to stone. Jennifer Dickson's superbly evocative photographs add to the overall power of the book.

The Amorous Unicorn (Porcupine's Quill, 1984) is Florence Vale's second collection of drawings and verse. Both the drawings and the verse are full of her good natured sensuality, but whereas the drawings partake, however lightly and wittily, of the modernist experiments in form, the verses tend toward the old-fashioned in both language and style.

The Amorous Unicorn is fun to read and look at; it's always enjoyable to read playful limericks and quatrains on sex. But only occasionally does Vale achieve the kind of utterly human acceptance of the life of the senses which her drawings imply. When she does so, it is usually in a plain and unobstructed syntax and near prose statement, as in "Skin":

> I can sleep with the excess of love
> Still damp on my skin.

In moments like these, the humane lover, who is also the artist, speaks without artifice, and it is these moments which give her book its value, however entertaining the light verses may be.

Jiri Valoch's *Haiku* (Underwhich Editions, 1983) is another of Underwhich's neatly presented tiny pamphlets of minimalist experimentations. Valoch, like George Swede, uses as few words as possible, but where Swede broke the very words, up, Valoch simply floats them free on the page, three words in three numbered lines per page. Now this is foregrounding the language-act with the vengeance, yet it's all so understated we might miss the potential significance of the meditative effort involved. There's even a narrative *in potentia* here, as the possible perceiver acts on the environment of water and sky. Like so many such minimalist works, *Haiku* can either be easily dismissed at a glance or else entered into as an opening to the reader's imaginative journey. As I enjoy the latter possibility, I think it's a sneaky and likeable little book.

In reviewing David Waltner-Toew's first book, I suggested that his was a humane and friendly vision; nothing in *Good Housekeeping* (Turnstone Press, 1983) alters that observation, for his new poems, especially those of his own or others' domestic lives, continue to make a strong case for the middle way of loving kindness, generosity, and proper relations with others. The title of the new book nicely reflects Waltner-Toew's major concerns. In the first section of the book he writes of getting up in the cold early morning to prepare coffee, shopping, rolling his first pie crust, and the joys of having children. His dedication to his mother, "who taught me to wash the dishes with dignity," perfectly catches the tone of his most attractive poems. Here is a man, raised a Mennonite, aware of the truths of feminism, and faithful to those of his past, ironic but not cynical, and genuinely in love with the natural world around him.

The work poems in the second section, even when they speak of the lack of dignity in the job described, maintain their generous appreciation of life. Nevertheless, a slight didacticism creeps in which becomes a grave fault in the political poems of part three. It's not that I disagree with Waltner-Toews about El Salvador or "The Nazi Victory," but that the rhetoric is strained, the poetry sacrificed to the message.

A series of poems on the death of his father are truly affecting in their simplicity, and a group of love poems, though a bit too sentimental in language at times, is saved by its sense of the comic. In the last section, Waltner-Toews tells of his Mennonite roots in Manitoba. He's at his best in the personae of different generations as the cultural drift from faithful farm to godless city occurs. The same complaints in a new context make for rich human irony.

Waltner-Toews has a gift for natural metaphors but too often he weakens them, turns them into similes. There were times I wanted to tighten the poems just a bit more. On the whole, however, *Good Housekeeping* lives up to its title, offering its readers a warm and cosy vision that has the integrity of something worked for and therefore earned.

In *Counting the Hours: City Poems* (McClelland & Stewart, 1983), Tom Wayman tells us of his poetry: "Like my City, my poems are rambling / talkative, anecdotal: / their own existence the point of it all. / They are workmanlike, only occasionally inspired, / but each day solving the myriad of problems / necessary for production — which is to say, / what keeps us all going." This is a good description of what Wayman offers in this, as in his other volumes. Wayman is preeminently the personal essayist of the workplace, as his editing of anthologies of work poems, his writing of a collection of "essays on the New Work Writing," *Inside Job* (Harbour Publishing, 1983), and his many poems on the subject demonstrate. Others may deal with Eliot's big three topics (or were they only Sweeney's?), but Wayman insists on the need to explore the fact *and the value* of work in his works (and he is fully cognizant of the pun and its implications, merely insisting that poets too should engage the problem, along with everyone else).

It's hard to fault Wayman on his theme, nor do I wish to, for he approaches it fully aware of its complexities and confusions, as "Asphalt Hours, Asphalt Air" (previously published in *A Planet Mostly Sea*), and many other poems demonstrate. He is also right to suggest that what happens in the work place affects friendship, love, creativity — all those things poets traditionally write about, and him, too. But he wants his work to *do* something, *work for* others, and he is upset when other writers fail to try as he does to do that:

> When someone writes
> there is a light in the leg of a hen
> that is the same light Moses saw
> as a pillar of fire crossing the Sinai by night
>
> I am filled again with the weariness
> that plagued us all those years on the Left.
> What help have these words been to another person
> that anyone should believe what they say?

A part of me agrees with Wayman when he says these things, as he does in *Inside Job*, but another part wonders if, as has often been argued, the artist's duty is not to art, to create beautiful and truthful images which enter our lives, even if they don't immediately change or explain them. Wayman must sometimes wonder, too, for some of his poems appeal to such visions, and they are often the most traditionally poetic in language, rhythm, and tone (but that may be ironic, a comment on their implicit failure to reach the ordinary folk he so often celebrates).

So I'm brought back to Wayman's own description of his poems and my basic response to it and to them. I take great pleasure in reading Wayman yet I find I read him more as an essayist than as a poet. Except occasionally, as in "Privacy Poem," "Long Beach Suite," and "Five Births," where his language takes on a tension and intensity, I find lacking elsewhere in this collection. These poems continue to speak to his primary concerns but they also begin to sing.

In *From the Songs of the Artisans* (Fiddlehead, 1983) Liliane Welch has set herself in a complex and interesting task: to pay homage to various people of various crafts through her own. The objective is noble, especially as all but the "Healers" and those she chooses to call "Diviners" (scientists tracking bird migrations) are working in ancient and personal technologies. Nevertheless, I believe her very awareness of the archaic roots of some of these crafts leads her astray in pursuing the demands of her own.

In many of these poems, Welch provides a system of allusions to poetry or speech as metaphors for the particular crafts she celebrates. On the whole this works well, for all the people she honours seek to communicate with others as well as with "the other" of their material. In many of the poems she adds another layer of allusion, this one to ancient myth, mostly Greek. Too self-consciously sign-posted for their own good, and occasionally somewhat off base (I fail to see the relevance of Icarus to the biologist's tracking of tagged birds), these tend to get in the way of the often precise descriptions of the actions the crafts demand of their followers. And in one case, that of the Woodturner, the reference to a dryad introduces a sexually violent sub-text I don't think was intended.

For me, the best group of poems is that for the Loggers. Here Welch sticks to perceived facts and acts in the known landscape of New Brunswick. The result is a sharp and precise imagery that matches the poet's photographs with their laconic iconography of the real.

David S. West, like Douglas Lochead, has chosen to write of war, but not his war; rather the war honoured in *Trenchmist* (blewointment press, 1984) is the Great War which his father fought in and later told stories about to his son. West says "these poems are a form of narrative documentary, poetic story-telling if you will, set in the mind of a WWI veteran, looking back on his involvement in what was the first thoroughly modern, mechanized, and technological war."

Part of the value of these anecdotal poems is the way they register the forms of mechanized and technological destruction which confront the various voices in the poems. West has obviously done more than just listen to his father; he has researched the war, and then he has subsumed his research in his invention. The poems present men on parade, on detail, in battle, drunkenly recovering from battle, and during the long, boring hours in the trenches when nothing happens. In all these situations, West captures both the horrors and the awful comedy of the Front. Indeed, the narrators have bitterly sharp senses of humour as they perceive the absurdity of their situations.

West writes in a loose open form, yet its laconic gestures seem suited to the characters and tales it records. *Trenchmist* is first a collection of stories, but it also posits some possibilities concerning the maturation of the Canadian character. All in all, it's a fine addition to the growing shelf of documentary poems.

Bruce Whiteman's early books were intensely lyrical in form and content. His most recent work has evolved "toward different sources and different concerns." Yet, as he confesses in a note to his *Recesses in the Heart: The Thera Poems* (blewointment press, 1984), the lyric impulse as "a body of knowledge . . . elicited not only these poems" but continues to persist in his ongoing fascination with "the flesh, the planets, and the whole archeology of individual memory." At any rate, there are moments of lyric intensity as well as lyric wit in *Recesses in the Heart,* even as its larger structure as a sequence begins to shift it away from pure lyricism.

Among other things, this is a collection of highly sensual love poems. What else would an Ontario boy write on the sunlit Greek island of Thera, about which Laurence Durrell said, "the reality is so astonishing that prose and poetry, however winged, will forever be forced to limp behind." Now that's a challenge, and Whiteman's response is to create an imagist lyric which slides toward comedy and thus points the way to the rest of the book:

> Cyclamen, anemone, oleander,
> white & purple flowers like
> daubs of paint
> on a
>
> dry
> broken landscape.
> Birds flying
> at the sun or
> dogging a
> slow fly,
> swooping low to the
> swish of a
> donkey's tail.

The comic vision implied here applies equally to the natives and tourists, the strange sounds of the place, and the necessary inward turn to erotic love, which is heightened by the lovers' sense of their alien presence in this lush landscape.

But then the lyric does tend towards lovespeech. And the poems take their chances with that language, despite the potential for pretentiousness and sentimentality, both of which Whiteman wittily acknowledges, and thus averts. He also acknowledges the question of inheritance, but he never forgets that the act of poetry is an act of desire, and that language and our relation to it is the key:

> Nichol's pun
> that language
> is "lung wage"

> we work & return
> each night to sleep
>
> our returns are
> the words on our tongues
>
> things speak we
> strain to hear their
> music, "rock"
> from rock, "lip"
> from lip, each act
> & natural thing
> sing its sound
>
> round breath that
> lets us into the
> world of stars & men

Of course, any poet who quotes Nichol is going to win my preliminary assent; but Whiteman keeps me interested with his wit and precision, his sensual speech and comic self-awareness. These poems range widely while preserving their core vision. In their range and variety, they argue well for Whiteman's continuing growth as a poet. *Recesses in the Heart* is a delightful introduction to his work.

Fugue Brancusi (Sono Nis Press, 1983), the latest and surely one of the most powerful and concentrated words by J. Michael Yates, is a perilously inviting black hole of a text. Savagely austere in its intellectual deconstruction of the works of intellect, it is full of emotional time bombs as only a spiritual quest in an animal body can be. The poem simultaneously creates and destroys the structures of thought and feeling it explores; it is a nexus of paradox, as are the works of its heroic progenitors Bach and Brancusi, as is the art of improvisation which it celebrates.

Each "section" of *Fugue Brancusi* is a two page poem of individual lives whose relation to each other is something akin to the relationship between couplets in a ghazal. The vocabularies of cosmology, law, photography, art, love and other fields of endeavour feed the ongoing Statements and Variations. Each line in each section has a koan-like presence, asking the reader to pause and meditate, yet one is called on, possibly to make connections, possibly to discover that the connections refuse to be made. Toward the end of the "Third Movement," the text makes these problems clear, but refuses to attempt to solve them: "The I was never I, you see, because of its problem serially, / And either: what I have lived, I have not written; / Or: I have lived every flaming line; / Or: the inexact universe whorls on inexactly / From more to most inexactitude, / The worse expressed by my crude orrery." This conjoining of macro and micro universe casts it shadow over all that preceeded it, the lines which appeared to float free of any personal voice, and those which appeared to be heartfelt cries of a particular individual. The poem is a voice in a textual void which is not empty space but rather the too full space of intertextuality, where we all live and speak, whether we know it or not. Yates knows it, thus all these various, usually closed, vocabularies jostling for room in the poem.

Fugue Brancusi invites contemplation, the pure aesthetic response, with marvelous power. We are not asked to accept but to receive its continually shifting linguistic perspectives. For those readers willing to accede to its demands, it's a text of continual openings.

Patricia Young begins her first collection, *Travelling the Floodwaters* (Turnstone Press, 1983), dealing from strength: it's hard not to want to read on when the first couplet of the book is "how should i speak to the crows / when they subtly ostracize mama." The poem and poems which follow do not always live up to the comic, absurd, wit of these opening lines of "Mama and the Crows," but the neatly askew imagination they signal makes itself felt often enough to create an engagingly strange volume.

Young sometimes tries too hard to set up metaphoric shifts of focus (sometimes running her similes into the ground, as in "Daughter"), but when she settles into her most spirited and precise mode, that of storytelling, she can create some disturbingly sensitive psychological monologues, like "When Looking for a Man." Young's personae are usually caught up in archetypal love or family relationships, and she makes this possibly too psychiatric approach in her best pieces because of a precision of tone and a wicked sense of humour. Her less successful pieces usually falter on pretentious allusions or a kind of forced surrealism in the analogies. But the good poems outweigh the poor ones, and the energy of her imagination and wit speak well for her continued work. *Travelling of the Floodwaters* introduces a talent I suspect we will hear from and delight in again.

"Comparing the wing, or the heron, / to an angel I construct a mystery," says Carolyn Zonailo in one of the poems in *the wide arable land* (Caitlin Press, 1981), and the whole book manifests her desire to construct mysteries by making arcane analogies which mix mythology and the natural life of the B.C. coast where she lives. The book opens with a selection of short lyrics, of which "Heron," the poem in which those lines appear, is the best, but Zonailo really comes into her own in the poem sequences which follow.

In "Sonnets of Despair" she constructs little nightmare scenes, mostly of a domestic nature. "The Red Camellias" is a black fairy tale in which a wound is a thing to be passed from hand to hand, and four allegorical figures dance a strange pavane of art and practicality, love and disillusion. In "Annunciation, the angel," Zonailo continues to weave the mythic into the profane, using the Bible story to engage Charles Olson's statement "that the social is economic / and that the political is ethical." Then in "Ceremonial Dance" and "Journey to the Sibyl" she pushes her exploration of archetypes further into the mythic past, all the while anchoring her dream quests in the local landscape of the West Coast and the lives of the people who live and work there.

Not everything succeeds here; sometimes Zonailo seems to be straining her analogies. Nevertheless, the highly Romantic imaginative explorations Zonailo practices here (and it's no accident her title comes from Keats) are courageous and often highly provocative. There is much in *the wide arable land* that calls our imaginations into action.

In her Preface to *A Portrait of Paradise* (blewointment press, 1983), Carolyn Zonailo says, "The task, for the poet, is to render the actual experience with as little artifice as possible," which could be taken to signal a greater clarity and simplicity than she sought in her previous book. Well, yes and no. The first poem here, a sequence titled "Blue and Green," is a phantasmographic exploration of images of power, violence and love, all inherent in the ocean. But she also seeks a "moon without / metaphor" in another poem from the "Landscapes" section.

In "Portraits," especially in a series of poems which deconstructs the idea of a female nude from a feminist perspective, she specifically calls into question many of the mysterious images of conventional Romantic perception. These poems are in fact portraits of paradise lost in misunderstanding. In the "Songs" which follow, however, Zonailo begins to close in on terrestrial paradise. These poems celebrate, with a compassionate stark simplicity, the world as it is experienced. Illumination and lucidity are key terms here, and the poems achieve them in "a spasm of grace."

The final section, "Mandalas," contains reproductions which fail to do justice to the original paintings they are based on, but which, with their suggestive titles, point to a wholeness that vision always seeks. In these, as in the best of the poems, especially the songs, Zonailo comprehends without dissipating in explanation the paradoxes life continually presents us. This is a not unworthy achievement, and it is perhaps as close to *A Portrait of Paradise* as we can hope to get.

Zuk (Porcupine's Quill, 1982) is "Translated from the French of Georges Zuk, with an Introduction and Notes by Robin Skelton" — and a magnificent work of contemporary scholarship it is, too. Skelton has previously given us selections of Zuk's work in the *Selected Verse* of 1969 and *The Underwear of the Unicorn* of 1975, but now that Zuk's continuing poem has reached its end and thus the end of Zuk, Skelton has collected both previously published and unpublished Zuk in one volume. It is all a great deal of translation to be sure.

As both Skelton's scholarly apparatus and the poems themselves make clear, Zuk was a master of paradox, and applied his wayward vision especially to sexuality. Since to be Zuk is clearly not to be Zuk — or to be not Zuk — and since the poems are the clearest example of this simultaneous being and nothingness, Skelton has to be especially careful as a translator. Or perhaps not. Whatever, the results are greatly entertaining, though they tend to pall a bit if taken in too large a dose at one time. Nevertheless, the recurring figures of lovers and others, the almost innocent clarity by which the poems present fetishism, and the often witty epigrams provoke both laughter and thought.

Professor Skelton's learned apparatus greatly enhances the whole, for it is obviously the result of many years' burning of the midnight oil and not a few Canada Council travel grants. All his effort is certainly worthwhile, for the scholarship is magnificent. Zuk lives as his poems if not in them. If we are to believe him he would have it no other way. A strange poetic turn for anyone, this book, this Zuk.

APPENDIX: LONGSPOON PRESS POETRY BOOKS

The title poem of Stephen Bett's first collection, *Lucy Kent and other poems* (Longspoon Press, 1983), is a seventeen part discursive sequence describing his imagined encounters with an unknown woman poet whose name he found on a rejection slip left in a library book. The fable is a flexible and useful one, providing Bett with a set of stepping-off points for his speculations upon literature and society, including the off and on nature of human relationships in, for example, poem V, "the geometry of love" or poem XIV, "a deceptive language." The balance of the individual sections is well maintained and the style provides, in general, a satisfactory medium, though from time to time it does become overly dependent on the similar work of George Bowering. There is considerable formal variety in the collection, from the direct, meditative statements of "Preparation for a gift" ("How true it is that we need to be / close to the brink of language when / we speak now."), through narratives or quasi-narratives of differing lengths, the multiple-voice structures of "Under eye and ear" and "Claviers and asphodels," to some final experiments with Chinese ideograms, "Three characters," which still owe too great a debt to Ezra Pound to be of much interest in themselves.

The book contains some interesting anecdote poems, such as the sharply evocative "Travel poem":

> Dark motel.
> The old man snoring
> on the other side
> of the room
> is my father.

Yet his controlled casualness can also work against and weaken any effective tension in this form, as with the flat and merely prosaic "Marlon" or the Laytonesque "It's been a long time since I / last read your poems" in "Poem." Over all, the meditative statement probably shows best his strength as a writer, as in the carefully constructed "Return to Jeffers through Everson," in which Bett can speak with a moving and suddenly simplifying voice that recognizes and states a basic determination to face and somehow deal with confusion:

> There is no question but one
> needs always to get it right, some-
> how get in there & be moved.

The voice in E.D. Blodgett's *Arché/Elegies* (Longspoon Press, 1983) is strong and consistent, though — intentionally — not always clear, or at least easily to be followed and understood. The book as a whole is something of an intellectual adventure, heavily allusive in places, and based on a series of primary semantic questions that are never quite fully answered. It is certainly nothing new for a contemporary poet to be thematically concerned with the independent/dependent meanings of words, with language as such. However, it is particularly significant and characteristic of this set of poems that Blodgett's artistic drive should be that to "go / mute where words begin, where lines forced / into rock record, meanings speaking in stone" ("Arché! Arché!"), which has frequently been the mystic's way to encounter a meaning beyond the capacity of any words. This kind of concern with linguistic elements, that constantly moves toward and then away from the possibility of successful speech, is reflected by D.G. Jones with his comment on *Arché/Elegies* as "drenched" in "the pathos of distance," with Jones here quoting Michel Foucault, quoted in another text as a general epigraph by Blodgett — words within words within words.

Blodgett usually makes positive use of this over-riding concern with words in these poems, employing it as a practical limit and base for further proceedings, as in this image, for example, from "O Canada":

> snow as space falling,
> infinite end of seasons striking the void
> of somewhere saying *a*, Lucretian sound
> of snow intact.

The particular letter image line here becomes more explicit with his later reference to "a language looking back / to find its letter *a*, to undeclare" in "Totem for Emily Carr." The powerful negative form, subliminally stating "to ... declare," is continued and effectively summed up in the ante-penultimate "Epistre dédicatoire (epilogue)":

> to unname,
> approaching to say, "There are no names for this,"
> to send across the vacancy of space
> more epithets for God Who hides within
> the sun . . .

Indeed, the poet and his book remain hidden as well, to some extent, intentionally inconclusive, though forceful and challenging throughout.

   The collection *Spokesheards* (Longspoon Press, 1983) by Sandra Braman and Paul Dutton, while still formally a publication, is in no proper, or at least to-be-expected way, a book. It consists physically of fifty-eight 10 x 15 cm cards, colour coded blue and grey to identify Sandra (*Spokes*) and Paul (*heards*), containing a set of more or less continuous hand written poems. It is more a collected exchange of thematically or imagistically connected poems, rather than a sequence, or double sequence, and so requires either to be followed through fairly rapidly, to yield a fictionalized experience of the original exchange between the writers, or simply to be broken into, more or less at random, for two-part connections, such as (card 3):

Light is	alone
privacy	spinning
	together
a prayer wheel	
	(Dutton)
(Braman)	

Sometimes the links are somewhat looser and explored in greater detail, as (card 11):

whose power	within four walls/mirrors
faces	a person
him	infinitely in them
self faces	(Dutton)
multiply	
his	
illusions	
of space	
fill	
(Braman)	

Sometimes, it must be admitted, the links lead to a curious grotesquerie, as (card 21):

<table>
<tr><td>Tissue net</td><td>hand</td></tr>
<tr><td>cancer of</td><td>led to breast</td></tr>
<tr><td>feeling</td><td>learns</td></tr>
<tr><td></td><td></td></tr>
<tr><td>you're felt</td><td>the aberrant lump</td></tr>
<tr><td>matted into my</td><td></td></tr>
<tr><td>being</td><td>another tumor</td></tr>
<tr><td></td><td>natural</td></tr>
<tr><td>(Braman)</td><td>swells within you</td></tr>
<tr><td></td><td></td></tr>
<tr><td></td><td>wet hair</td></tr>
<tr><td></td><td>there</td></tr>
<tr><td></td><td></td></tr>
<tr><td></td><td>(Dutton)</td></tr>
</table>

In sum, *Spokesheards* provides a game that, while it should not be played too often, or too seriously, provides for a good amount of originality, both in substance and in style.

Anne Campbell's *No Memory of a Move* (Longspoon Press, 1983) is a refreshingly positive and substantial collection. It is introduced and supported by a number of clearly presented memory poems, such as "Old country painting" ("My grandmother's sister dressed all in black / with babushka and old country ways") and the eight part sequence "Pine poems." *No Memory of a Move* shows an effective control of word and thought in certain closely observed psychological studies, such as "Edging out" ("I am edging out / of the way I think / I like to look") or the delicately exposed study "The answer":

>   Spirit
> you see   in me
>   but
>   it's in you
>   I've detected
> . . . delicacy   spirit.

As well as these carefully gathered details and insights, there is also a simple, well controlled musicality in many of these poems, a deft prosodic use of line breaks and space-marked internal pauses to provide both a sustaining voice and the use of special emphasis, as in "Old Lovers":

> The best thing
> about old lovers   is now

when you meet them
on the street   you can
throw your arms around them
hug them   kiss them
hold them to pieces
no worries   now
they're
cousins   uncles
brothers

and sons.

The devices are certainly appropriate here, though in some of the last poems in the collection ("You're dumb," "Fall") the mechanical scattering of phrases seems to be used (or shown off?) merely for its own sake.

A few of the pieces deal overtly with the matter of writing itself ("Stones," "The bed is a mess of a dream"), but the book is not particularly directed to explore the meaning of meaning or the wordness of words. Anne Campbell does ask a general thematic question of her work, "what is this / constant memory   what metaphor is here," and answers herself with something of a riddle, "memory of an absence / no memory of a move" ("Pine poems 8, Memory of a move"), but her concern is a practical and not a theoretical one, constant throughout the collection, posited and answered by means of the individual poems.

Monty Reid's *The Dream of Snowy Owls* (Longspoon Press, 1983) consists of eight brief poem sequences, each independent of the others, except for a minor transition between the first, "January," and the second, "Après-ski." Their subjects tend initially to be naturalistic — cross country skiing, Reid's wife painting her finger nails — but soon shift in emphasis away from the base situation and move by startling leaps of metaphor through a series of improbably related associations. Each provides in its own way the skeleton for an expressionistic fable. The symbolic action of "My wife paints her fingers," for instance, includes, with casual disregard for normal connectives, an insane bandit "in the suburbs / of the hand" who becomes the hammer of his own gun, is remembered as standing in a U.I.C. line-up, observed cruising through "the bar-rooms of the nose," and finally disappears in a meditation upon profit and loss. The quality of invention here is continuously impressive, even if not always secured by a clear artistic relevance.

Some formal variety is provided in *The Dream of Snowy Owls* by a sequence in prose, "Mysteries of the Great Plains" (along with the teasing sub-title) "from the book by Monty Reid") and by a roughly biographical set of descriptions ("The pictures of [William Carlos] Williams"), given somewhat in the manner of dust jacket blurbs. The title sequence shows most consistently Reid's considerable lyric gift:

Slow wings.   The arrival
late in October, of snow.
It begins and you have
never learned to expect it
because nothing changes
fast enough.   Love,
wisdom, weather.
Owl on a pole.

As its title suggests, this final sequence is structured explicitly by means of dream-like associations — moonlit snow ("ii"), the dreamer dreaming of himself ("iii"), a stuffed owl "mounted . . . in the school library" ("iv") — and thus gains more solidity and objectivity than the seven others that precede it. It gives a satisfying close to a collection that otherwise sometimes loses itself in its own whimsicality.

If *Spokesheards* can be described as only minimally a book, it is tempting to call Wilfred Watson's *Gramsci x 3*, (Longspoon Press, 1983) maximally so. Although Watson's form is basically dramatic, the presentation is textual to the greatest degree. In brief, *Gramsci x 3* provides a particular and highly stylised exploration of three significant occasions in and about the life and martyr-like death of Antonio Gramsci, leader of the Italian Communist party in the 1920's and 1930's. A considerable amount of this "text for performance" is presented according to the Number Grid Poetry system of notation that Watson has previously employed, to combine a highly abstract set of patterning suggestions for the actors (or speakers) with a usually very simple, slangy dialogue. Watson's detailed staging instructions, however, especially in "Finding Tatiana," the middle section of the play, do provide a specific, even a restrictive, counter to the openly suggestive, improvisatory material of the first group of scenes, "The young officer from Caligari." The tension between these two elements persists through the final section, "The doing-to-death of Antonio Gramsci," that lays out details of his death in 1937 against a sometimes crudely explicit enactment of the Stations of the Cross.

The extended and continuously self-referential nature of these "texts" makes it difficult to give any samplings that would briefly capture and reproduce the distinctively stradled or multi-dimensional approach that Watson takes to his historical/political theme. Indeed, even so basic a critical notion as theme seems inappropriate as a measure to examine and evaluate such a composition as *Gramsci x 3*. The scenes function best, perhaps, as a kind of abstractly linguistic and quasi-liturgical meditation upon this area of recent history, rather than an exposition of it in any clearly recognizable sense.

Some Fittes and Starts (Longspoon Press, 1983) is the first of five parts of *The Fells of Brightness,* Jon Whyte's long poem-in-progress. The main title, as he explains in a carefully detailed (if somewhat fatuous) "Preface," is based on a translation from the Cree "Assine Watche," meaning "Brilliant mountains," the Rockies. The term "fell" also signifies, by means of a pun on its connotation in the craft of weaving, a folded edge of cloth, as "fitte" is also a term for hem mark, both together suggesting a raised ridge, of text as well as the mountains themselves. Whyte describes his overall structure in the poem as that of an "anatomy"; his own interpretation of this seems, with a few special emphases directed to the work at hand and, presumably, as yet to come, much the same as that presented in more general terms by Northrop Frye some time back in *Anatomy of Criticism.* The thought of Frye is quite relevant here since Whyte's poem, this portion of it anyway, provides in part a form of criticism as well as "text," directed to itself and some others — the seventh and final section, "Epeirogeny," he describes as a "parody [of] the old-fashioned post-modernists."

The anatomy of this first part of his poem is still too complex to be illustrated in any detail by quotations here; and, indeed, the effect of it is a kind of slow confusion, much careful preparation for something that has not as yet happened, with, however, a persistent feeling as well that the completed *Fells* is somehow faintly present, at least in Whyte's mind and in the tone of these *Fittes.* He uses two major methods of exposition: multiple inter-effecting word and phrase lists, and a loose four-stress line in the Anglo-Saxon manner. Sometimes these forms work solidly, sometimes not. Here is a typical selection from the fourth section, "Ranging":

The fields	our minds	moving back
our minds	at play	and forth
wander in	scattering	discovering
disparate	combinant	facts
cloven	conglomerate	and fictive
places	alluvia	appearances

A more closely integrated and self-contained group appears in the first section, "Sources":

"Take me to a mountain meadow," she dreamt
                spoke
                wrote
     (a clothed softness, like the pleached folds
     (concealing conception upsurgent mountains show;
     (the plaited stems of blossoms on her fingertips
                      (entangled)

Whyte employs a fairly flexible verse line in his two "Wanderer" sections. The second of these, which also uses a marked caesura, is generally rather lumpish: "Wherever I wander   — in valley, on fell — / I bear in my bedroom   a burden of memory / confounding my comfort,   confusing my dreams / thwarting my footfall   in heath and in hinterland: / etc." The first "Wanderer," though, sings with a fine lyric purity:

> Pied patches of snow lie in the meadows' lees,
> in streaks on screes where slides have coursed, . . .
> in dappling flecks, in lakeside depths,
> in windshadows of the snow-tormented trees.

These discrepancies are characteristic of the volume. Yet the best of the writing clearly shows the chance of more fine things ahead, and the breadth of the material in *Some Fittes and Starts*, even if not always its particular articulation, suggests a substance sufficient for the poem-to-be as a whole.

INDEX OF PUBLISHERS